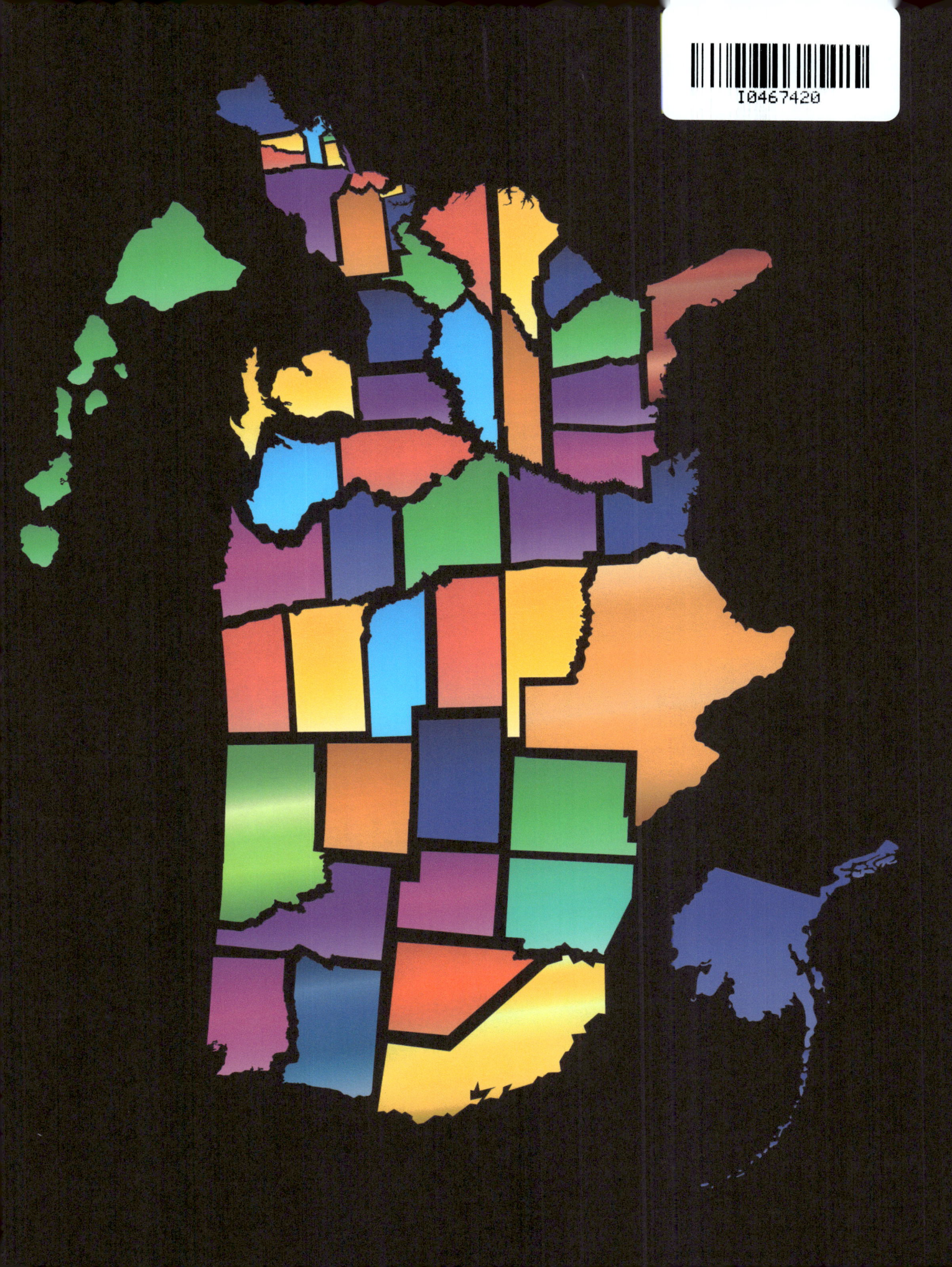

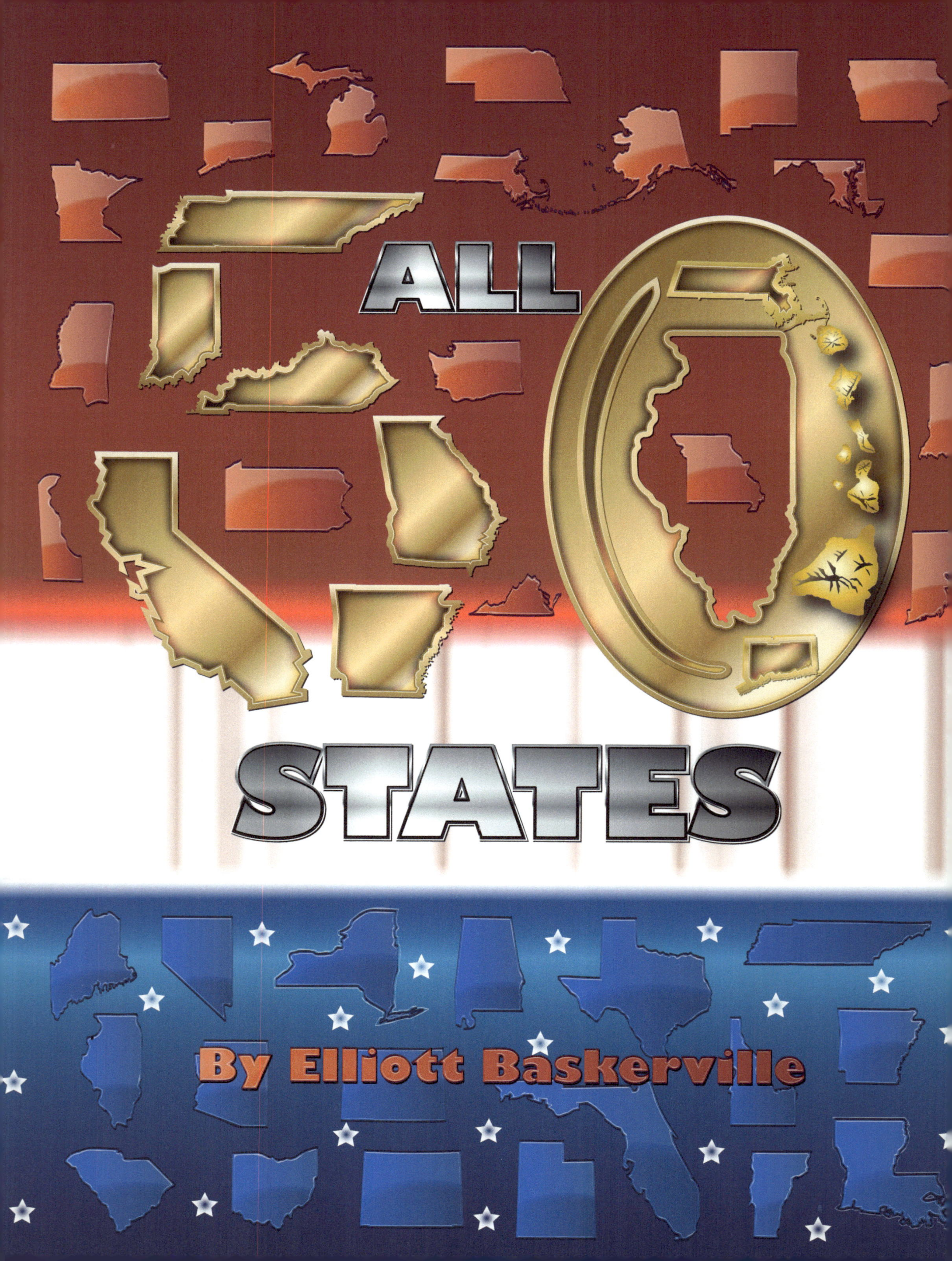

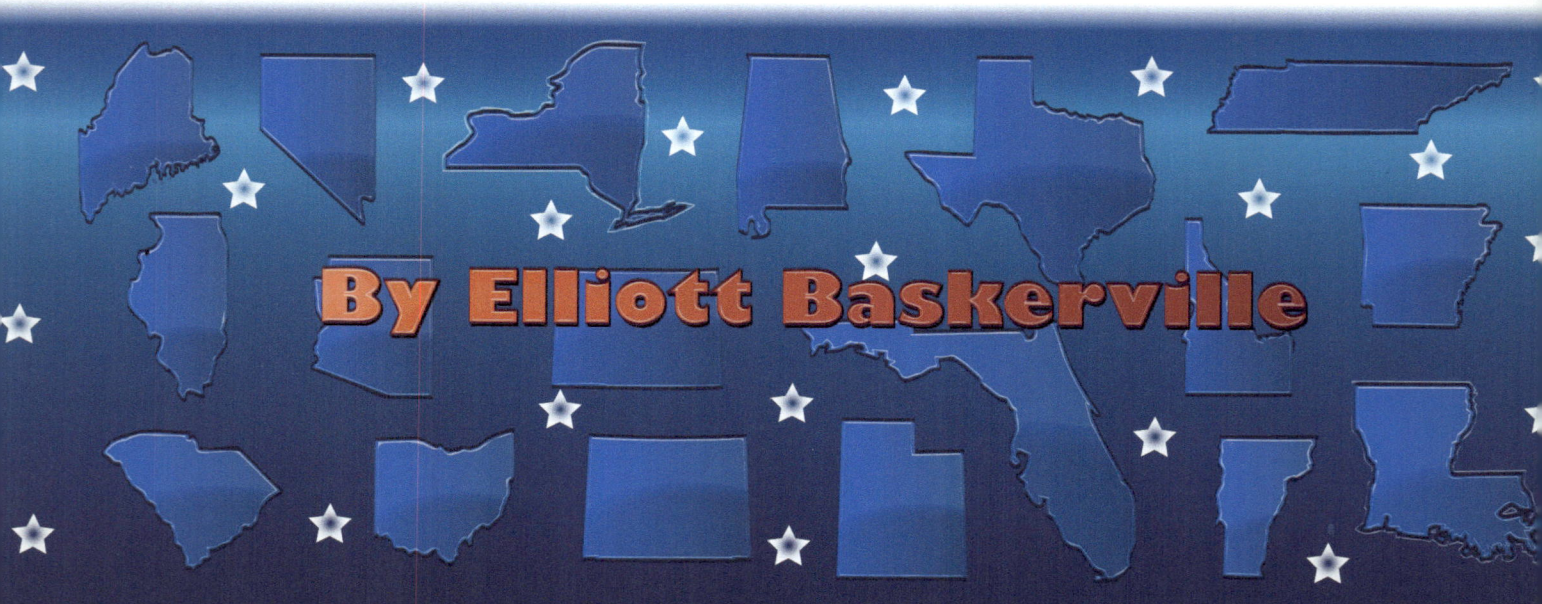

ALL 50 STATES

By Elliott Baskerville

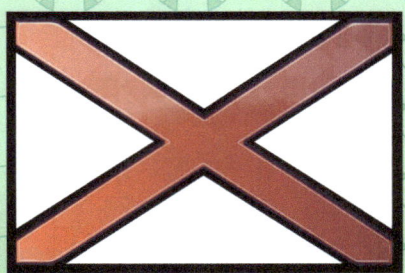

- Auburn
- Birmingham
- Decatur
- Dothan
- Hoover
- Huntsville
- Mobile
- Tuscaloosa

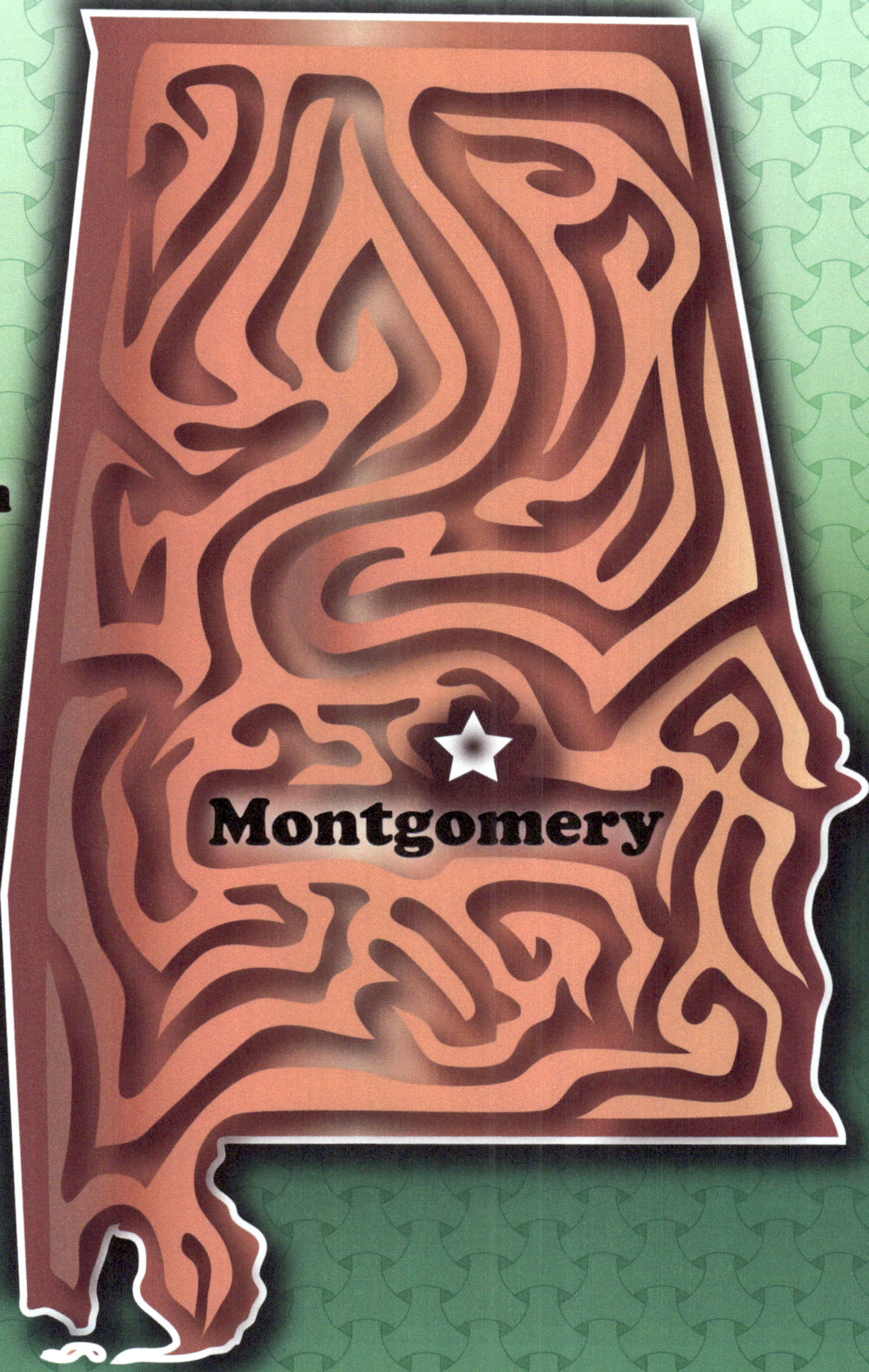

★ Montgomery

(AL)

ALABAMA

1

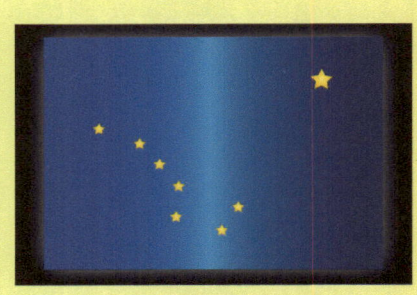

Juneau

- **Anchorage**
- **Badger**
- **College**
- **Fairbanks**
- **Ketchikan**
- **Sitka**

(AK)

2

ALASKA

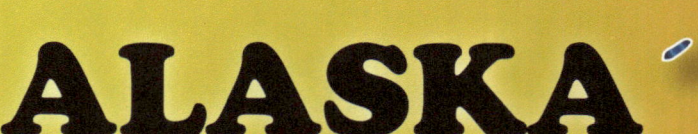

- Chandler
- Gilbert
- Glendale
- Mesa
- Peoria
- Scottsdale
- Suprise
- Tempe
- Tuscon

(AZ)

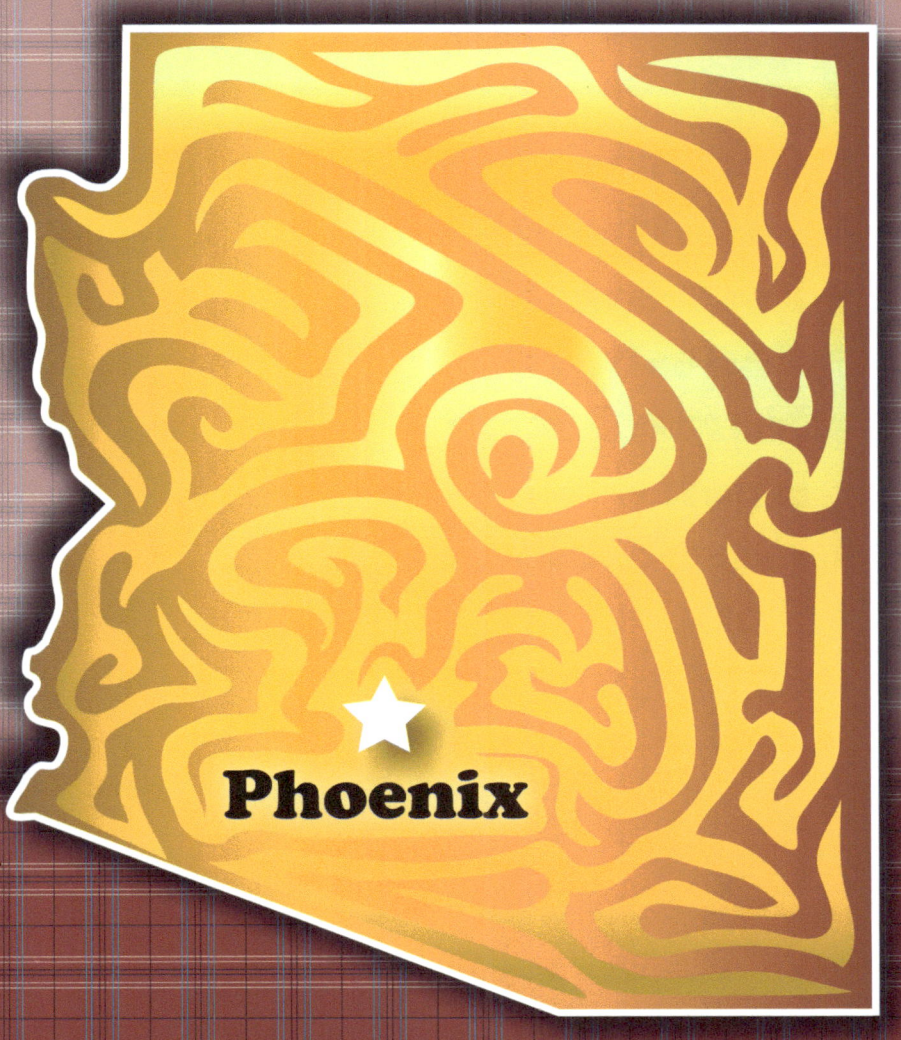

★ Phoenix

ARIZONA

3

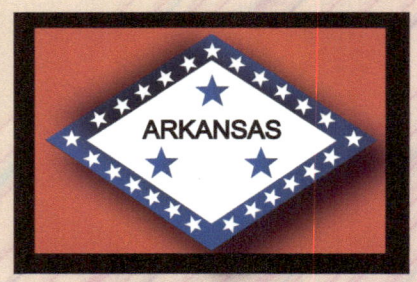

- Conway
- Fayetteville
- Fort Smith
- Jonesboro
- North Little Rock
- Pine Bluff
- Rogers
- Springdale

(AR)

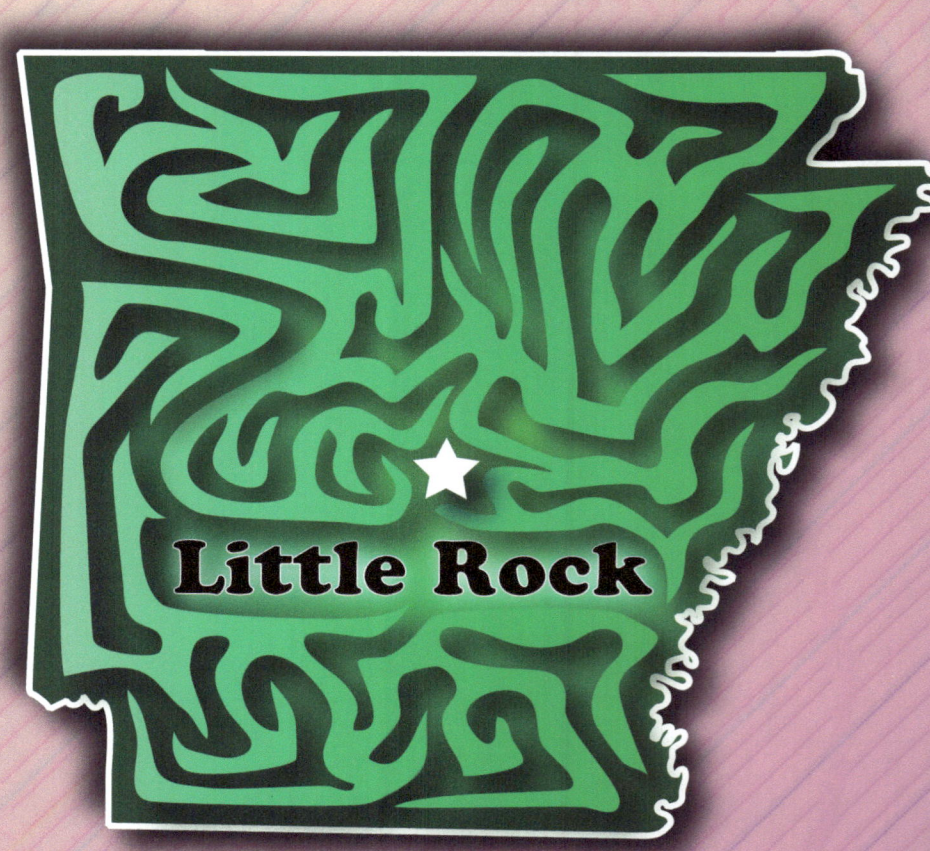

Little Rock

ARKANSAS

4

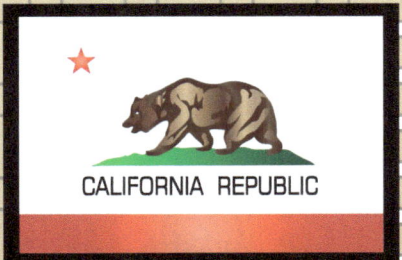

- Anaheim
- Bakersfield
- Fresno
- Long Beach
- Los Angelos
- Oakland
- Santa Ana
- San Diego
- San Francisco
- San Jose

(CA)

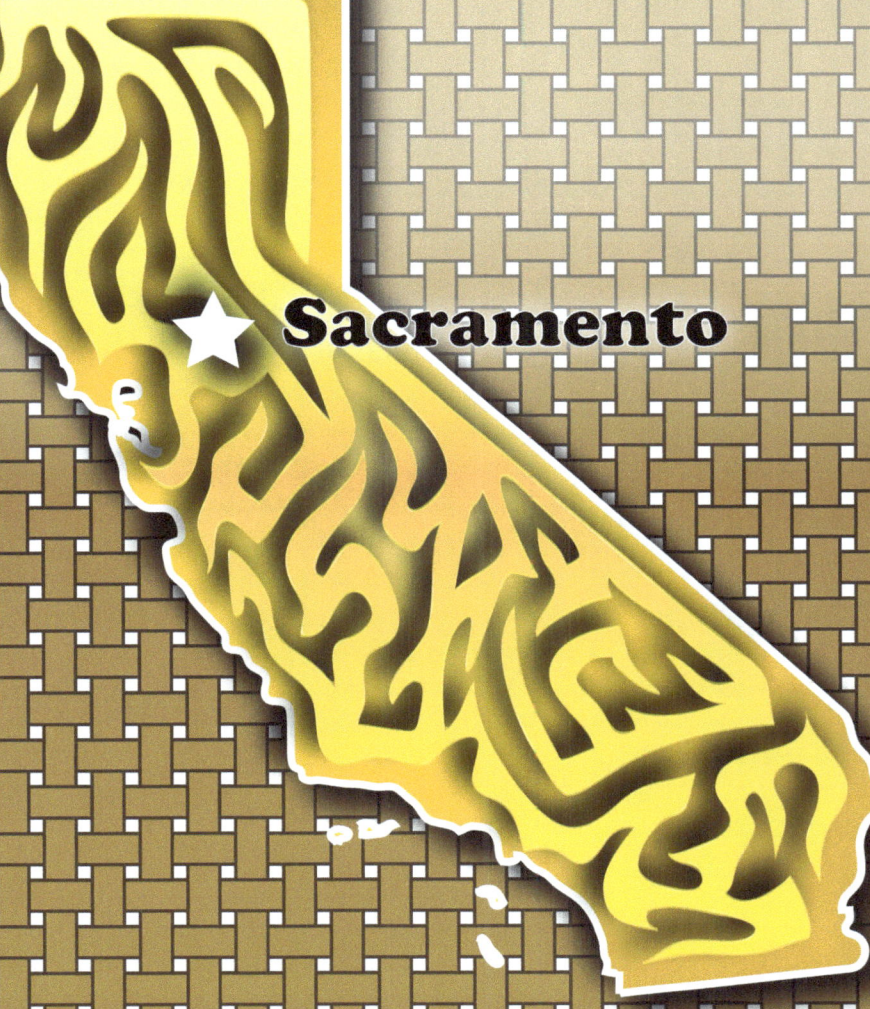

Sacramento

CALIFORNIA

5

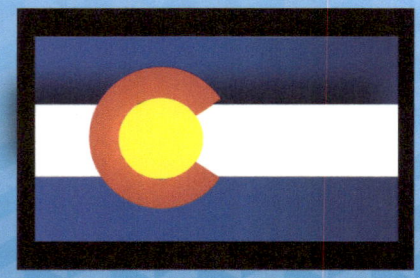

- Arvada
- Aurora
- Boulder
- Centennial
- Colorado Springs
- Fort Collins
- Highlands Ranch
- Lakewood
- Pueblo
- Westminster

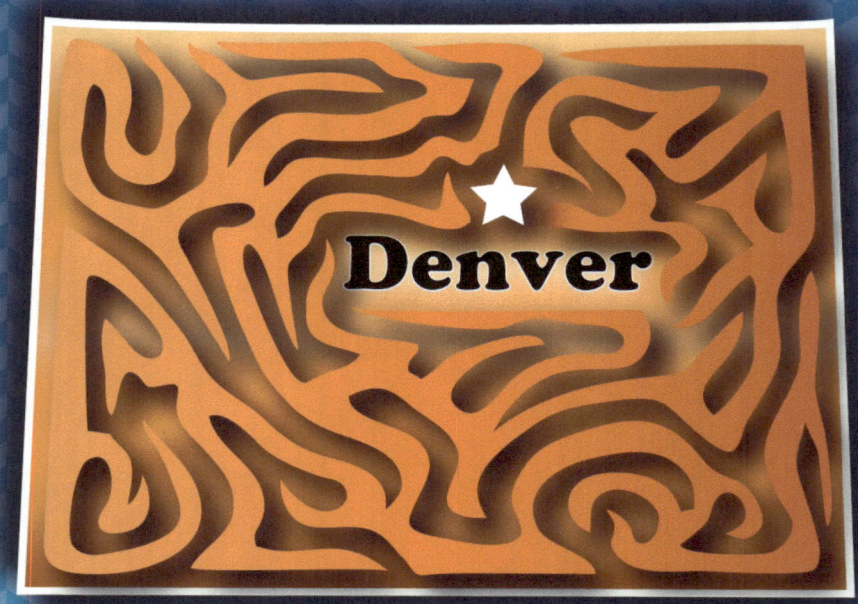

Denver

(CO)

COLORADO

6

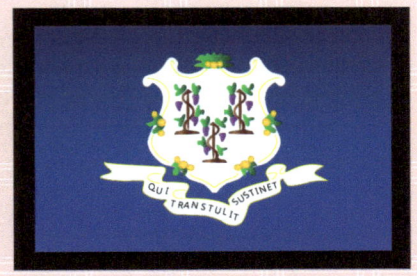

- **Bridgeport**
- **Bristol**
- **Danbury**
- **Meriden**
- **New Britain**

- **New Haven**
- **Norwalk**
- **Stamford**
- **Waterbury**
- **West Hartford**

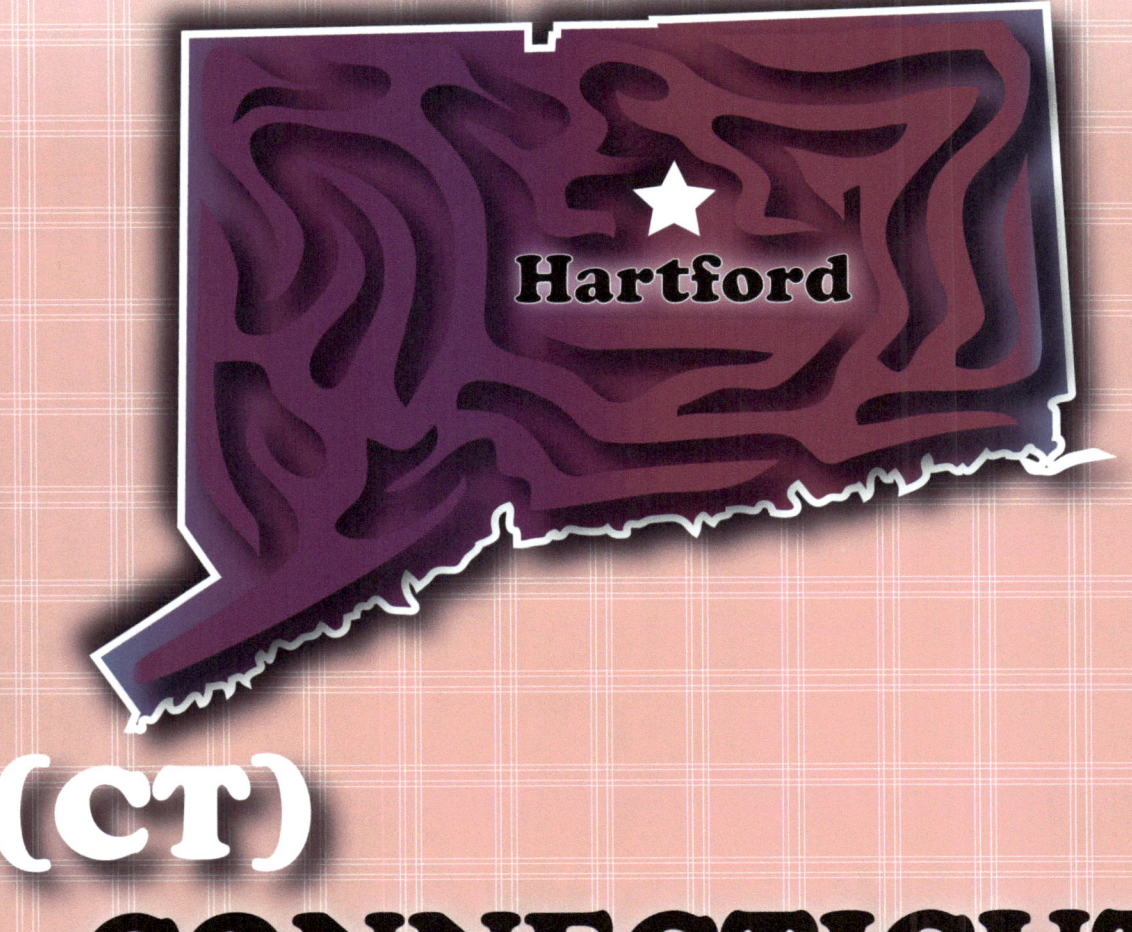

★ Hartford

(CT)
CONNECTICUT 7

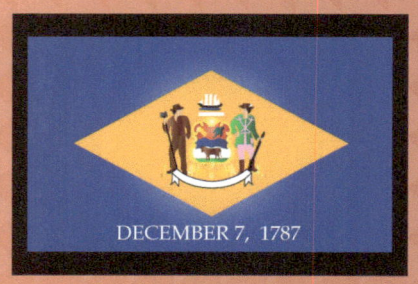

DECEMBER 7, 1787

- Bear
- Dover
- Middletown
- Newark
- Wilmington

(DE)

★ Dover

DELAWARE

8

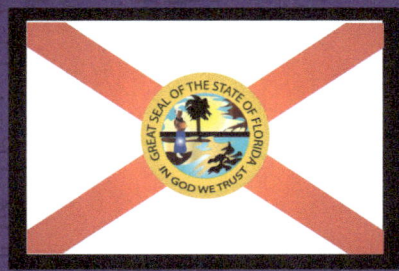

Tallahassee

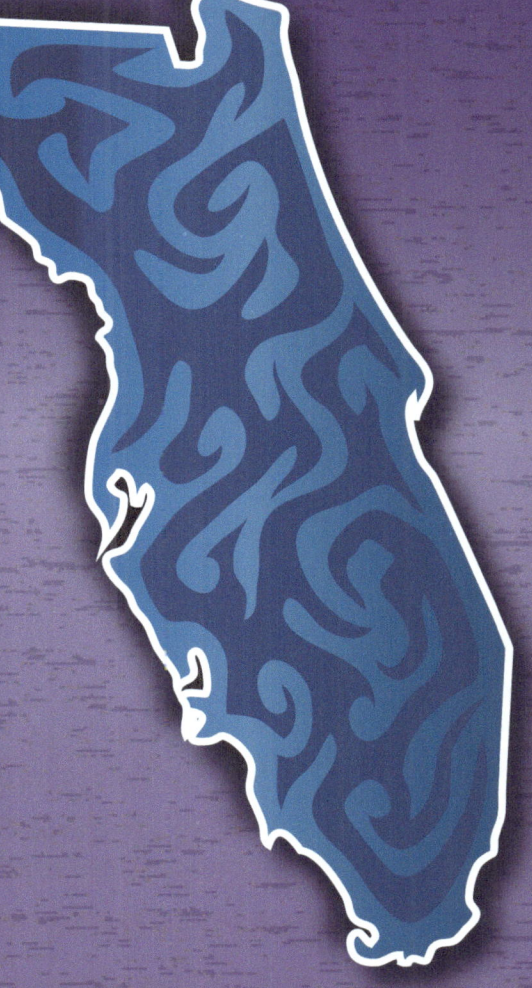

- **Cape Coral**
- **Fort Lauderdale**
- **Hialeah**
- **Jacksonville**
- **Miami**
- **Orlando**
- **Pembroke Pines**
- **Port St. Lucie**
- **St. Petersburg**
- **Tampa**

(FL)

FLORIDA

9

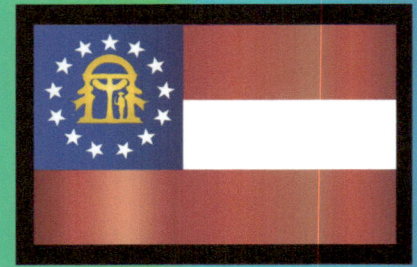

- Albany
- Athens
- Augusta
- Columbus
- Johns Creek
- Macon
- Roswell
- Savannah
- Pueblo

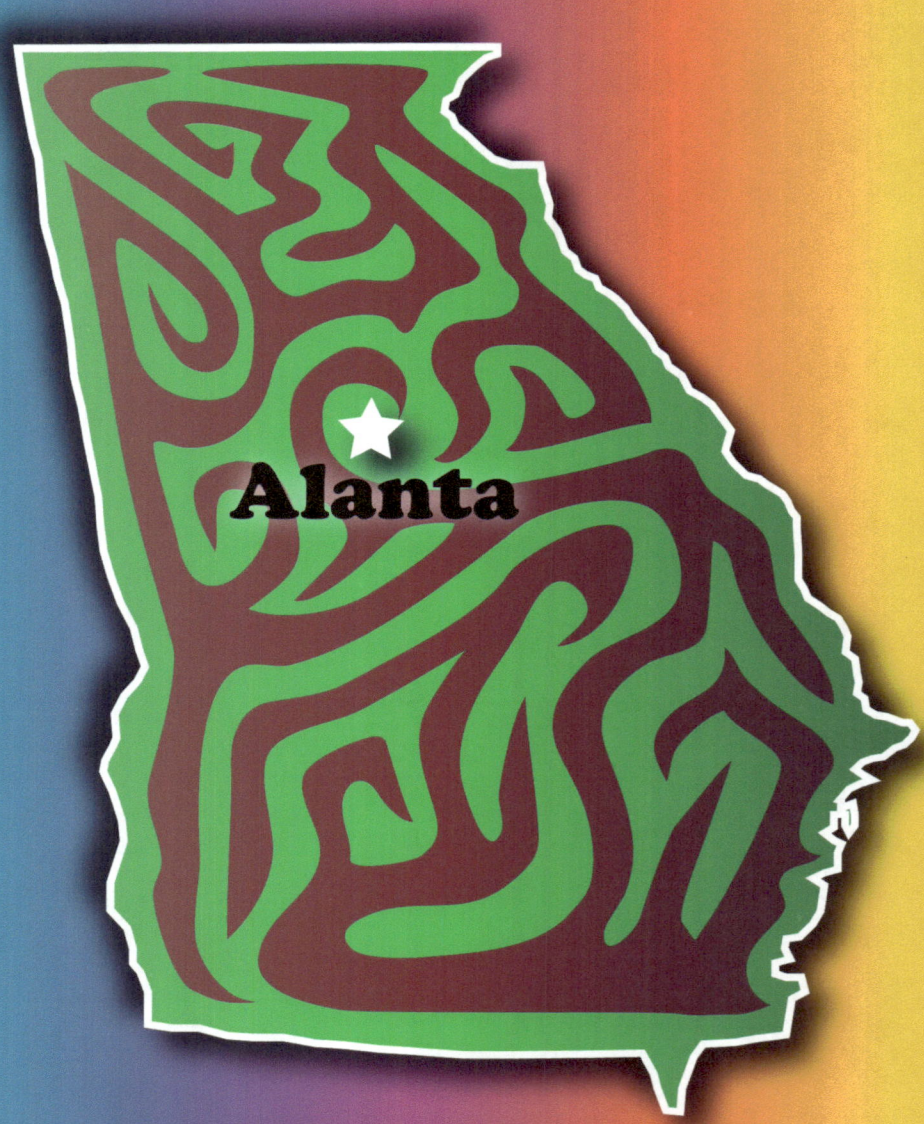

Alanta

(GA)

GEORGIA

10

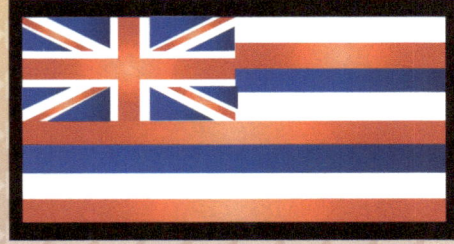

- **East Honolulu**
- **Ewa Gentry**
- **Hilo**
- **Honolulu**
- **Kahului**
- **Kailua**
- **Kaneohe**
- **Kapolei**

Honolulu

- **Kihei**
- **Makakilo**
- **Mililani Mauka**
- **Mililani Town**
- **Pearl City**
- **Schofield Barracks**
- **Wahiawa**
- **Wailuku**
- **Waipahu**

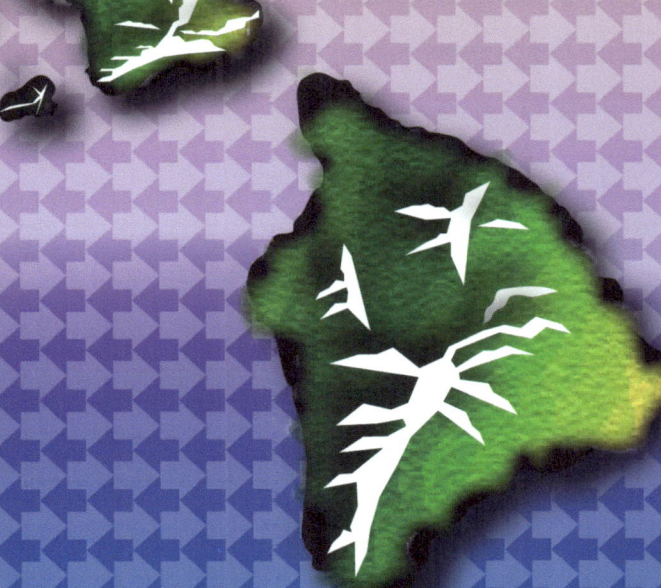

(HI)

HAWAII

11

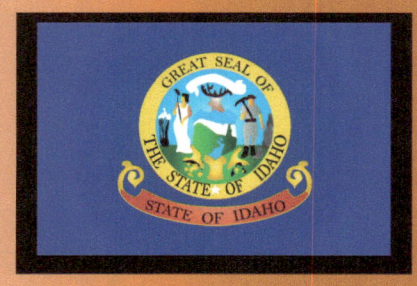

- Caldwell
- Coeur d' Alene
- Idaho Falls
- Lewiston
- Meridian
- Nampa
- Pocatello
- Twin Falls

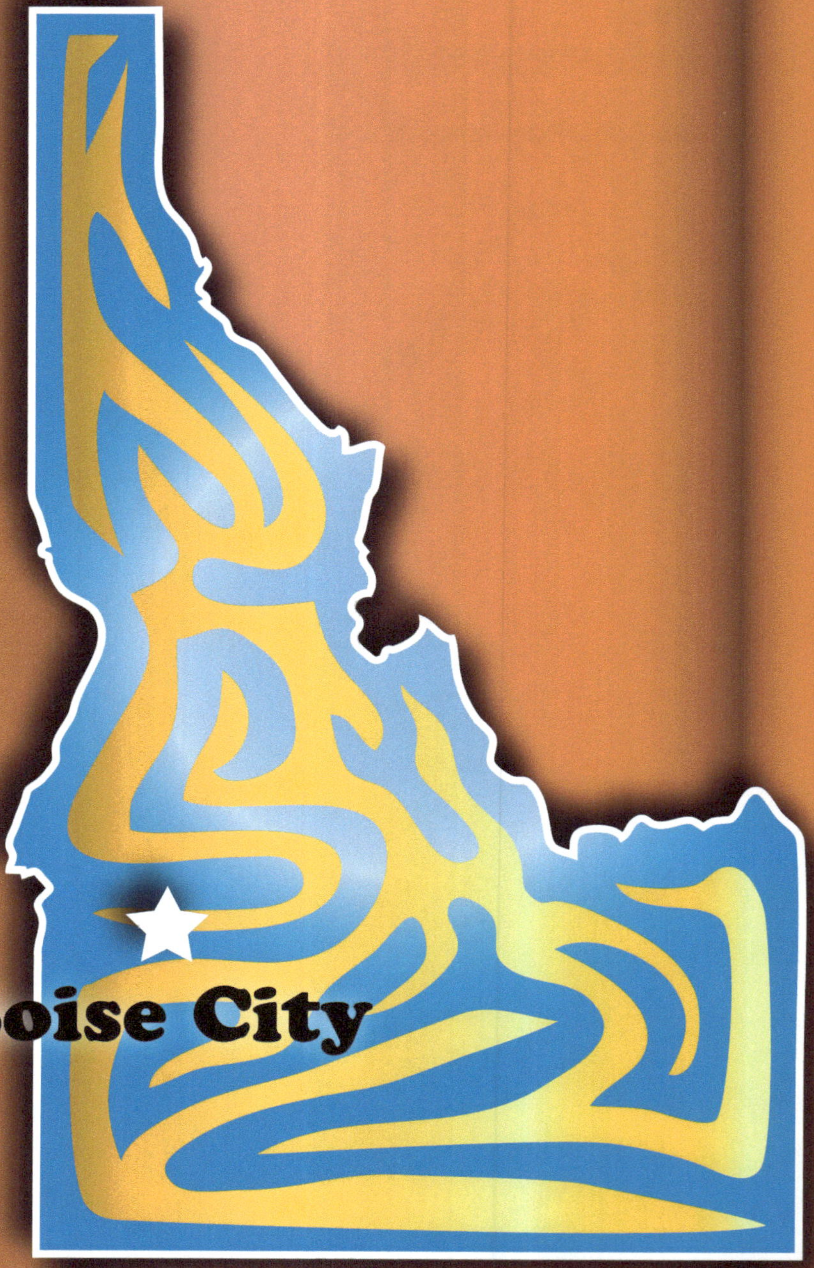

(ID)

Boise City

IDAHO

12

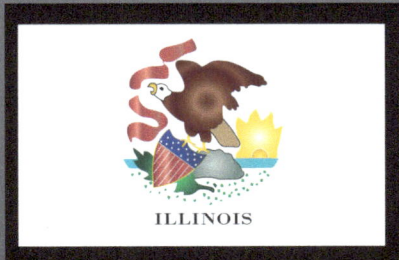

ILLINOIS

- Aurora
- Champaign
- Chicago
- Cicero
- Elgin
- Joliet
- Naperville
- Peoria
- Rockford
- Waukegan

(IL)

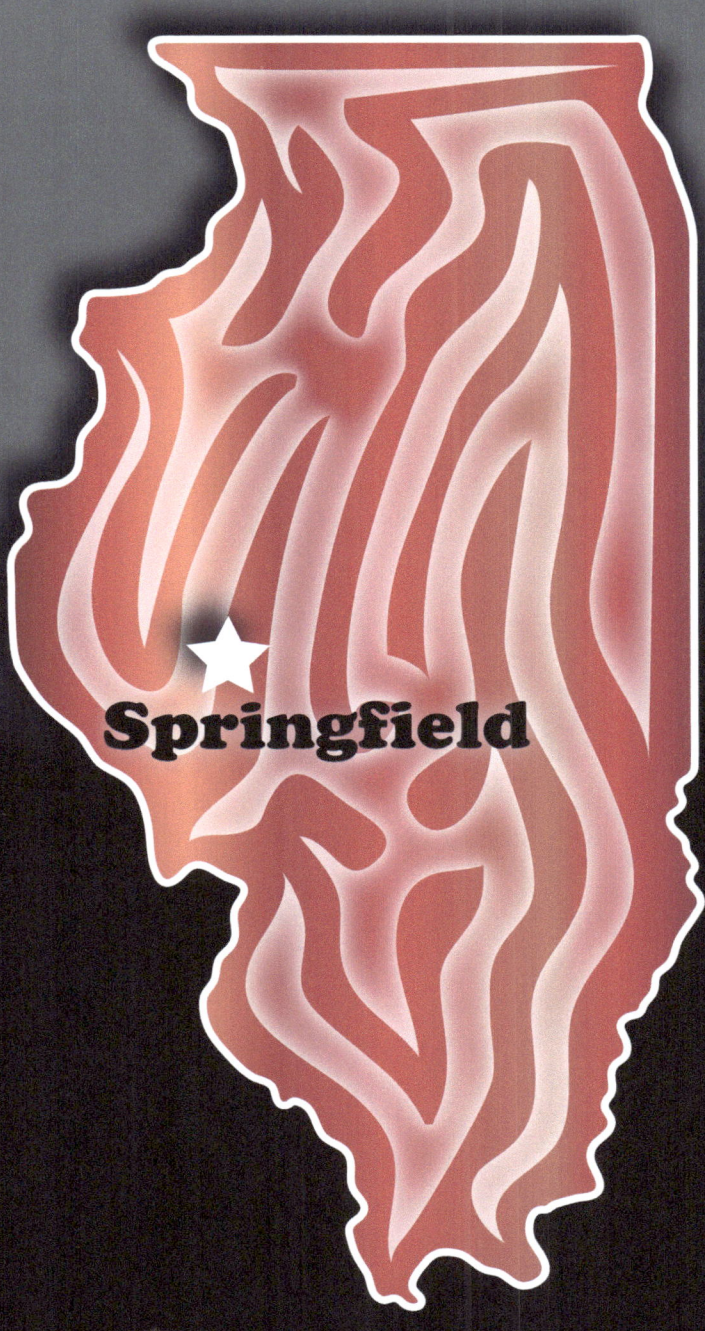

Springfield

ILLINOIS

13

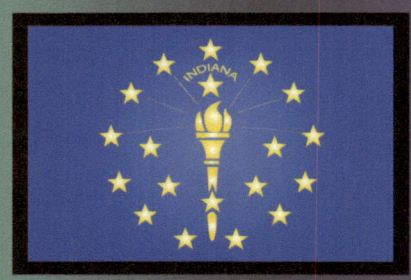

- Blommington
- Carmel
- Evansville
- Fishers
- Fort Wayne
- Gary
- Hammond
- Muncie
- South Bend

(IN)

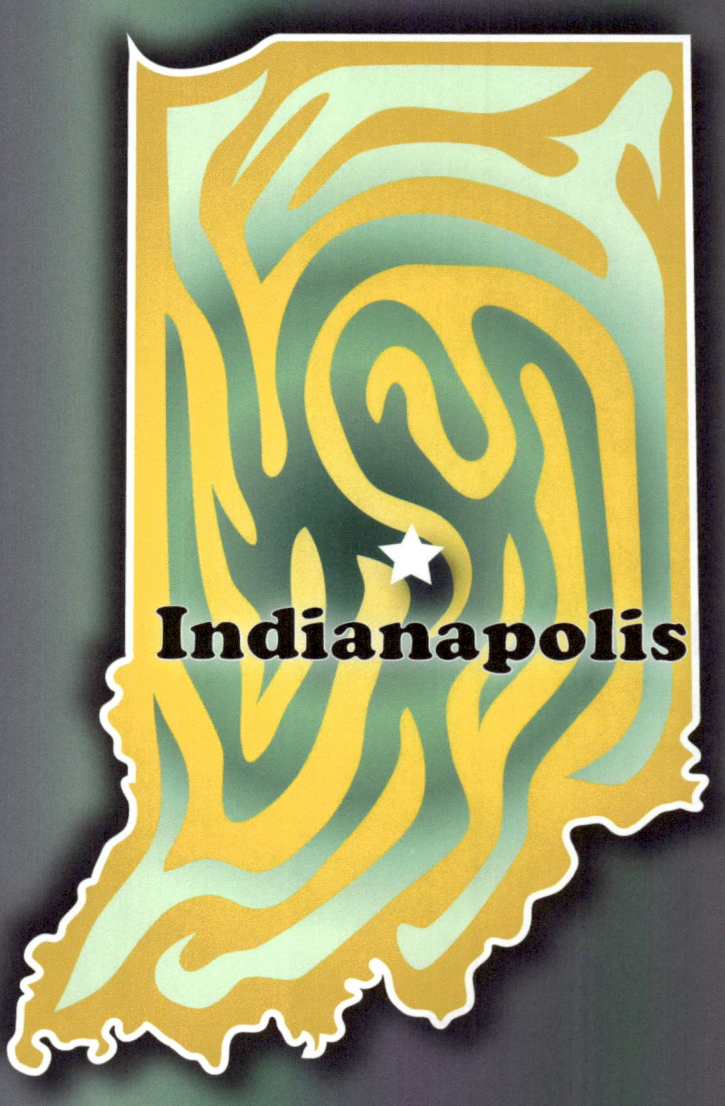

Indianapolis

INDIANA

14

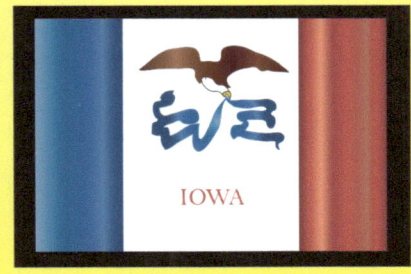

IOWA

- Ames
- Cedar Rapids
- Council Bluffs
- Davenport
- Dubuque
- Iowa City
- Sioux City
- Waterloo
- West Des Moines

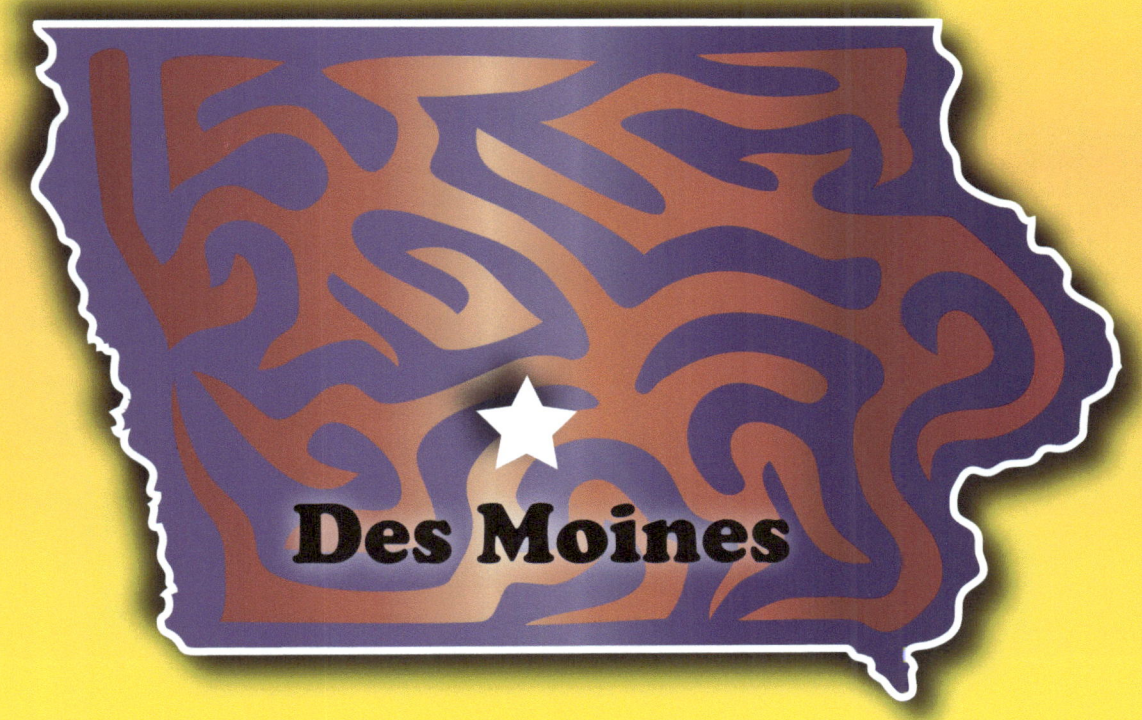

Des Moines

(IA)

IOWA

15

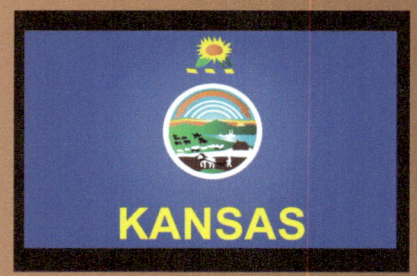

KANSAS

- **Kansas City**
- **Lawrence**
- **Lenexa**
- **Manhattan**
- **Olathe**
- **Overland Park**
- **Salina**
- **Shawnee**
- **Wichita**

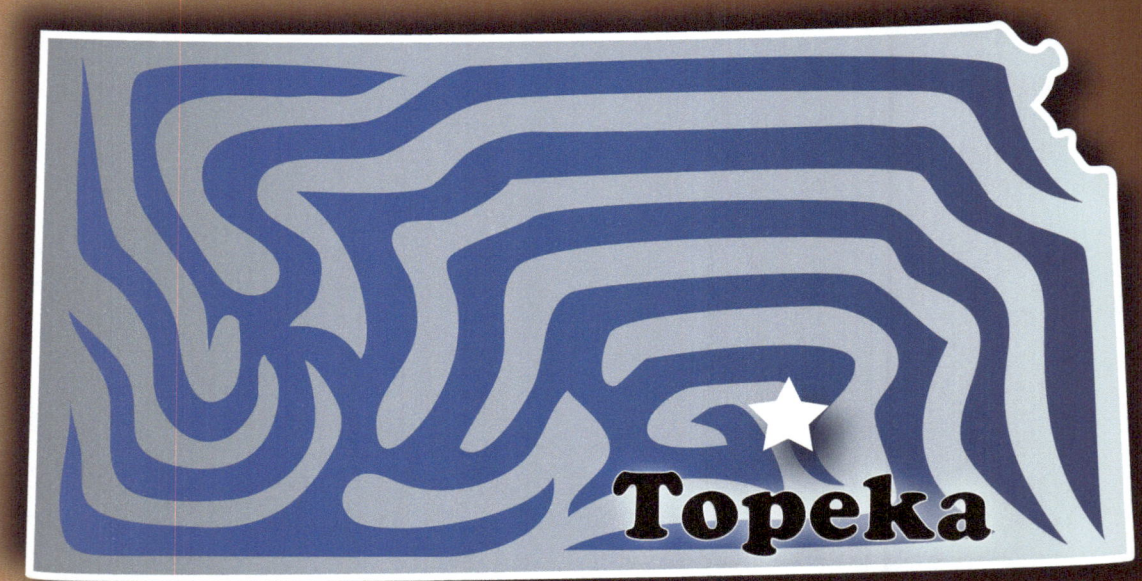

Topeka

(KS)

KANSAS

16

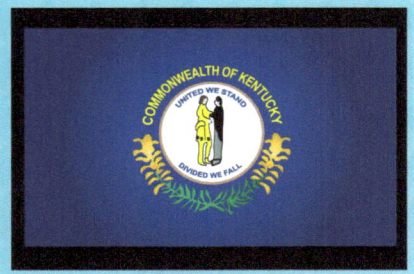

- **Bowling Green**
- **Covington**
- **Elizabethtown**
- **Florence**
- **Georgetown**

- **Hopkinsville**
- **Lexington**
- **Louisville**
- **Owensboro**

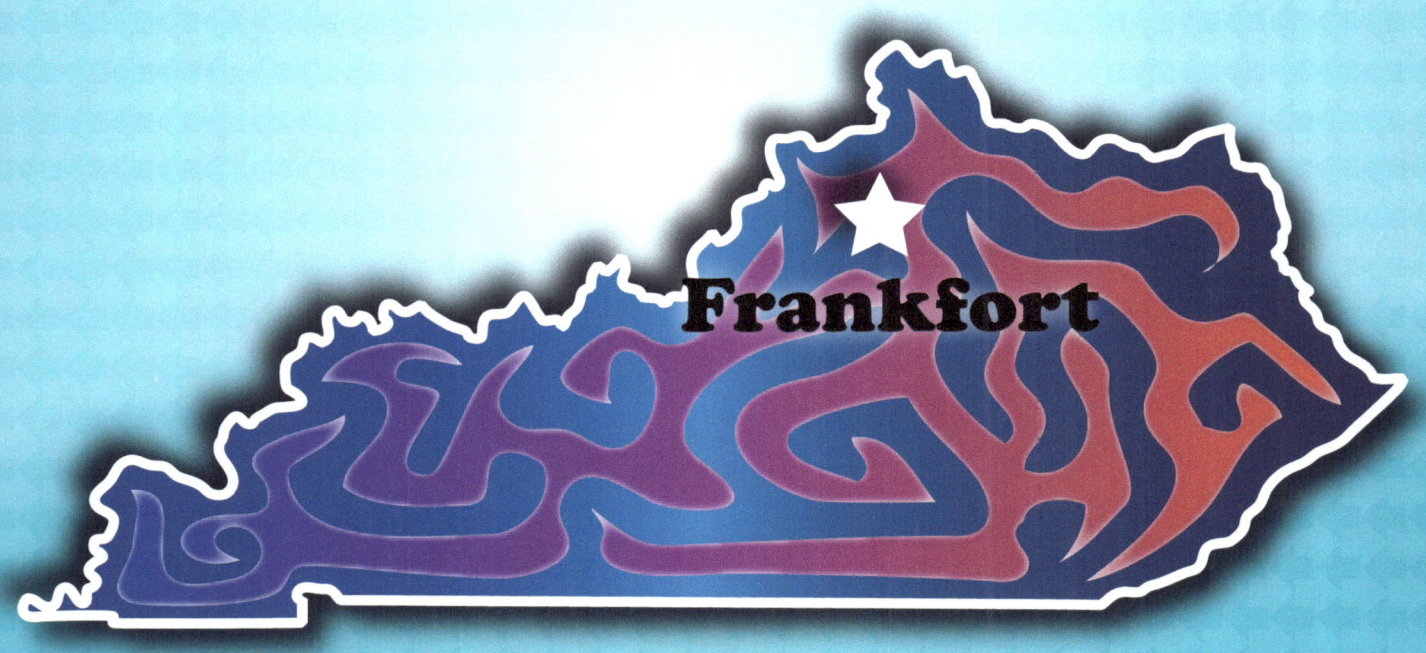

Frankfort

(KY)

KENTUCKY

17

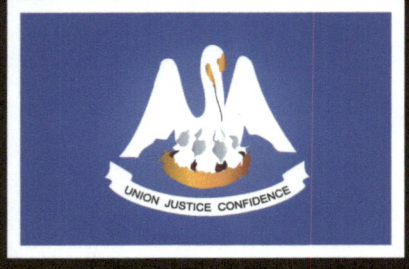

- Alexandria
- Bossier City
- Kenner
- Lafayette
- Lake Charles
- Metairie
- Monroe
- New Orleans
- Shreveport

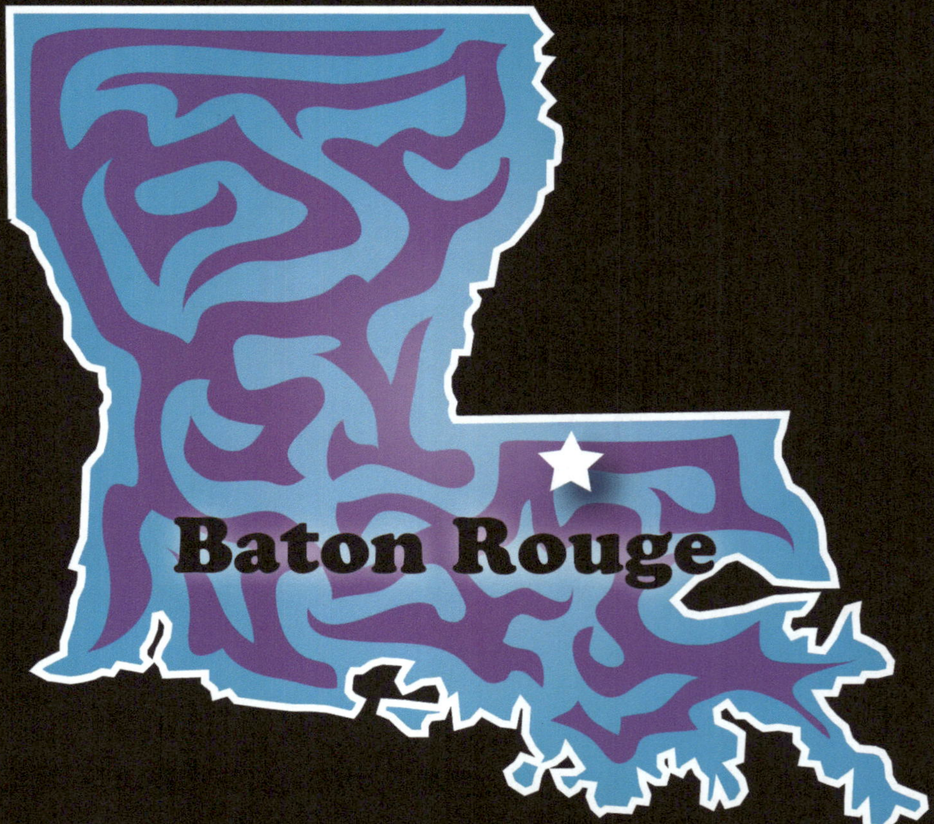

Baton Rouge

(LA)

LOUISIANA

18

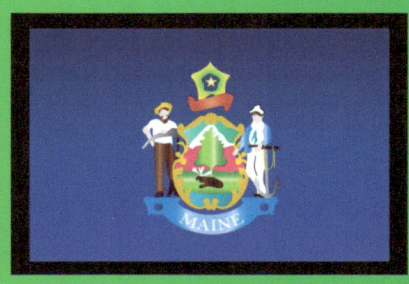

- Bangor
- Lewiston
- Portland

(ME)

★ Augusta

MAINE

19

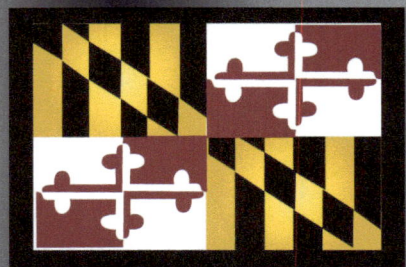

- **Baltimore**
- **Bethesda**
- **Columbia**
- **Dundalk**
- **Ellicott City**
- **Frederick**
- **Germantown**
- **Glen Burnie**
- **Rockville**
- **Silver Spring**
- **Waldorf**

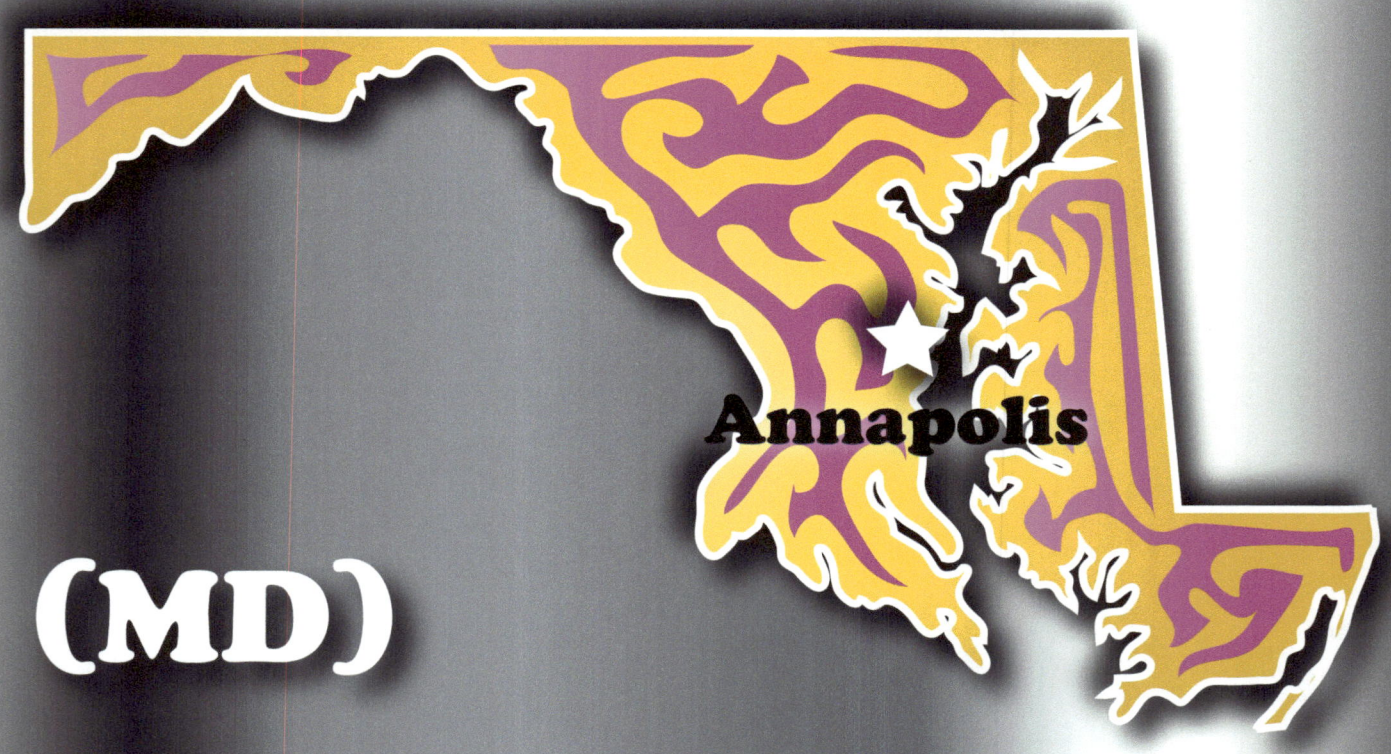

Annapolis

(MD)

MARYLAND

20

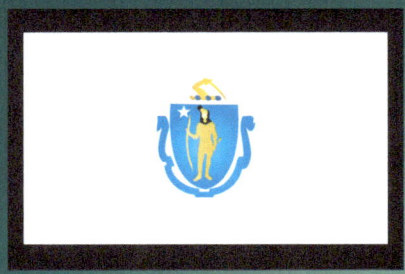

- Brockton
- Cambridge
- Fall River
- Lowell
- Lynn
- New Bedford
- Newton
- Quincy
- Springfield
- Worcester

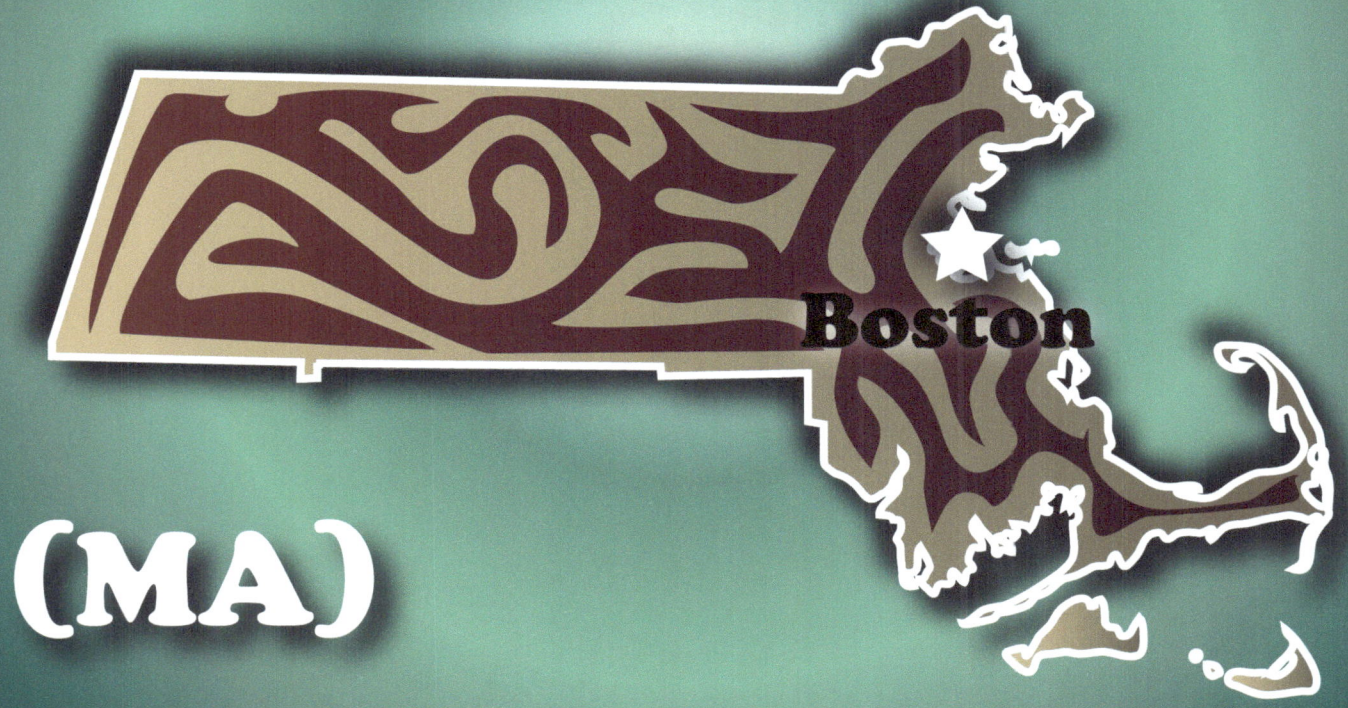

Boston

(MA)

MASSACHUSETTS

21

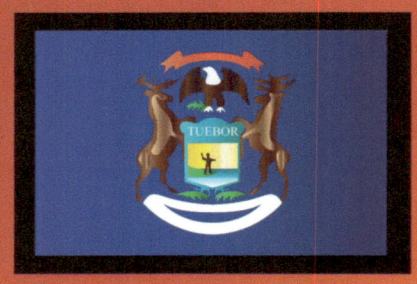

- Ann Arbor
- Clinton
- Dearborn
- Detroit
- Flint
- Grand Rapids
- Lansing
- Livonia
- Sterling Heights
- Warren

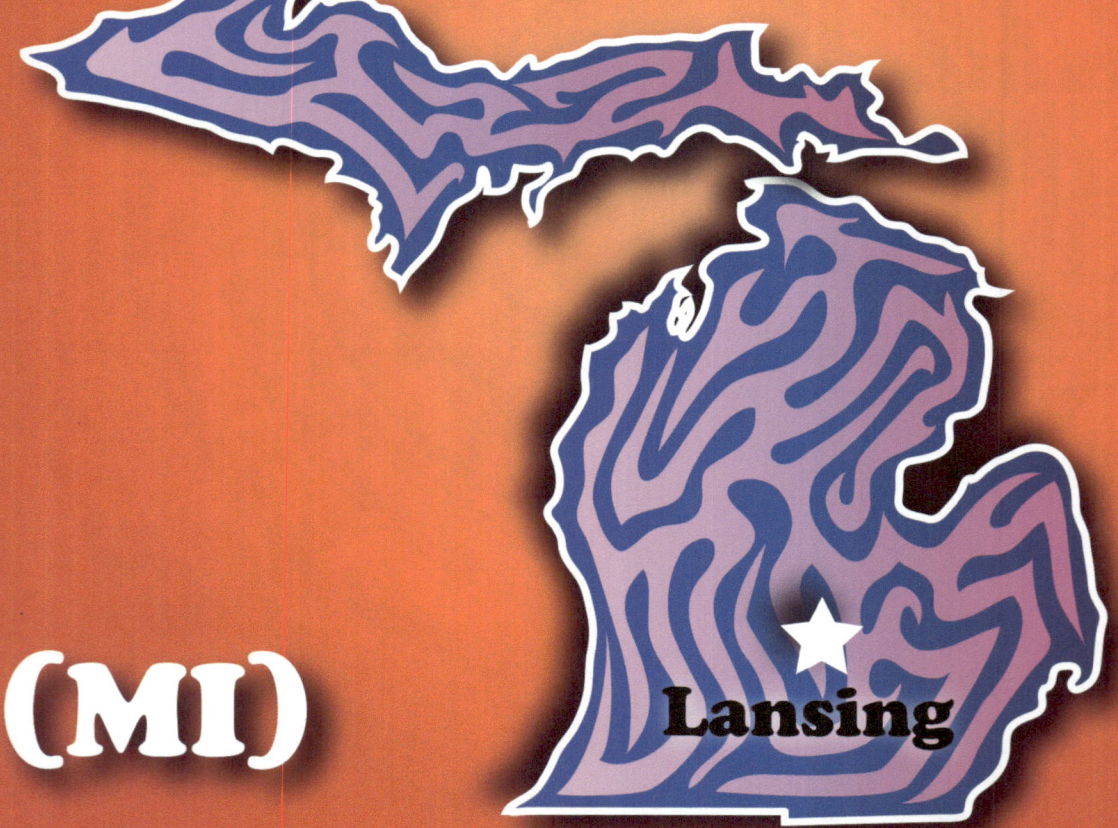

Lansing

(MI)

MICHIGAN

22

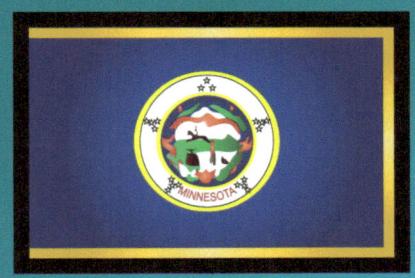

- Bloomington
- Brooklyn Park
- Duluth
- Eagan
- Eden Prairie
- Maple Grove
- Minneapolis
- Plymouth
- Rochester
- St. Cloud
- Woodbury

(MN)

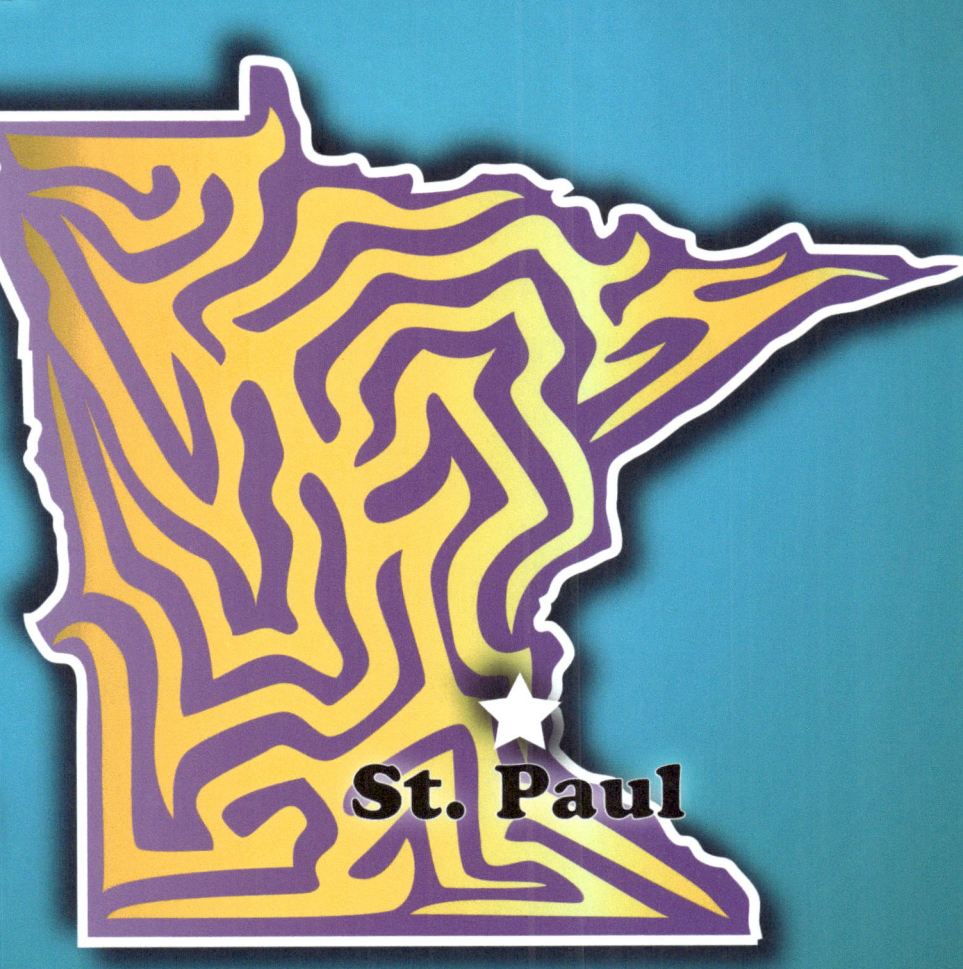

★ St. Paul

MINNESOTA

23

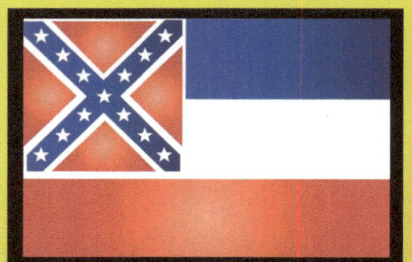

- Biloxi
- Greenville
- Gulfport
- Hattiesburg
- Meridian
- Olive Branch
- Southhaven
- Tupelo

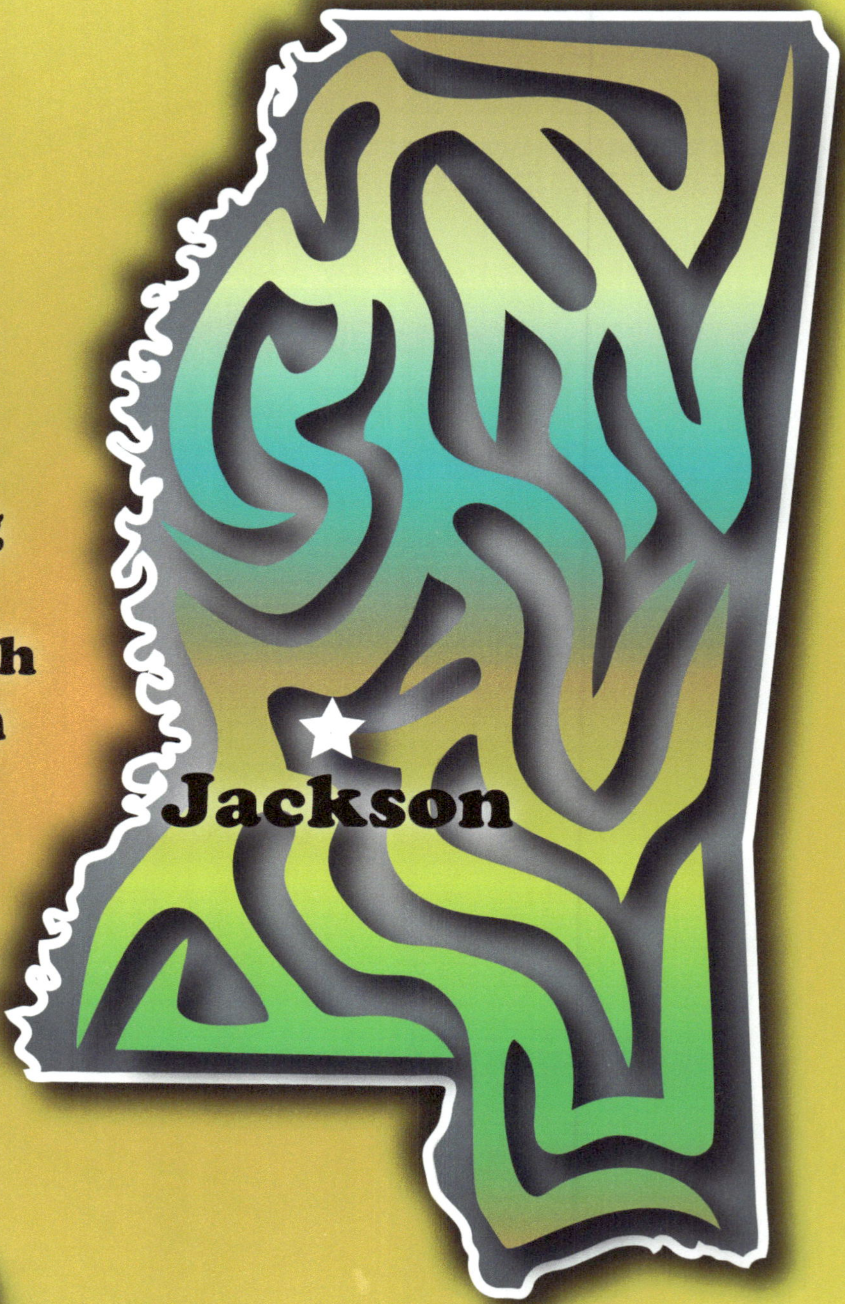

Jackson

(MS)

24 MISSISSIPPI

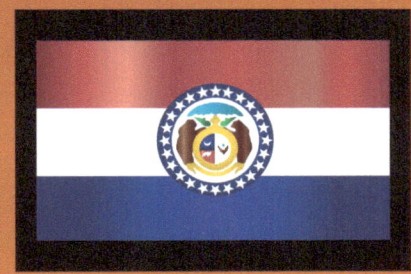

- Columbia
- Independence
- Lee's Summit
- Kansas City
- O' Fallon
- Springfield
- St. Charles
- St. Joseph
- St. Louis

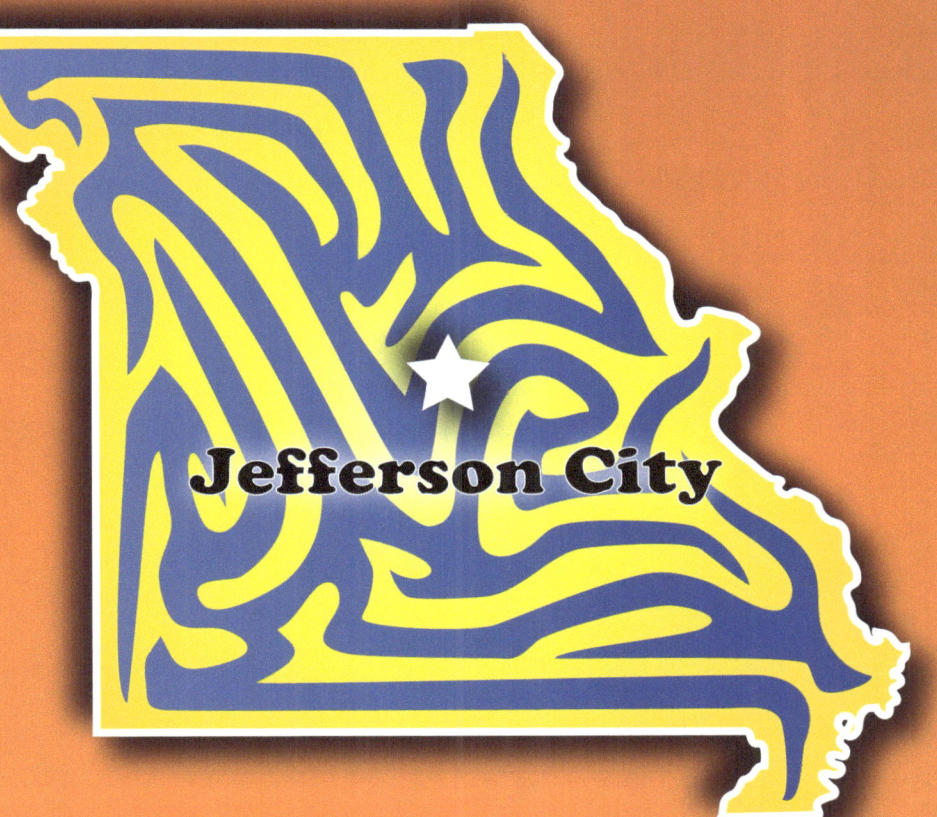

Jefferson City

(MO)

MISSOURI

25

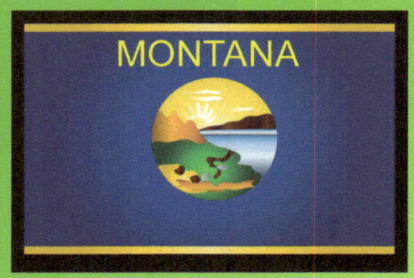

MONTANA

- **Billings**
- **Bozeman**
- **Butte- Silver Bow**
- **Great Falls**
- **Helena**
- **Kalispell**
- **Missoula**

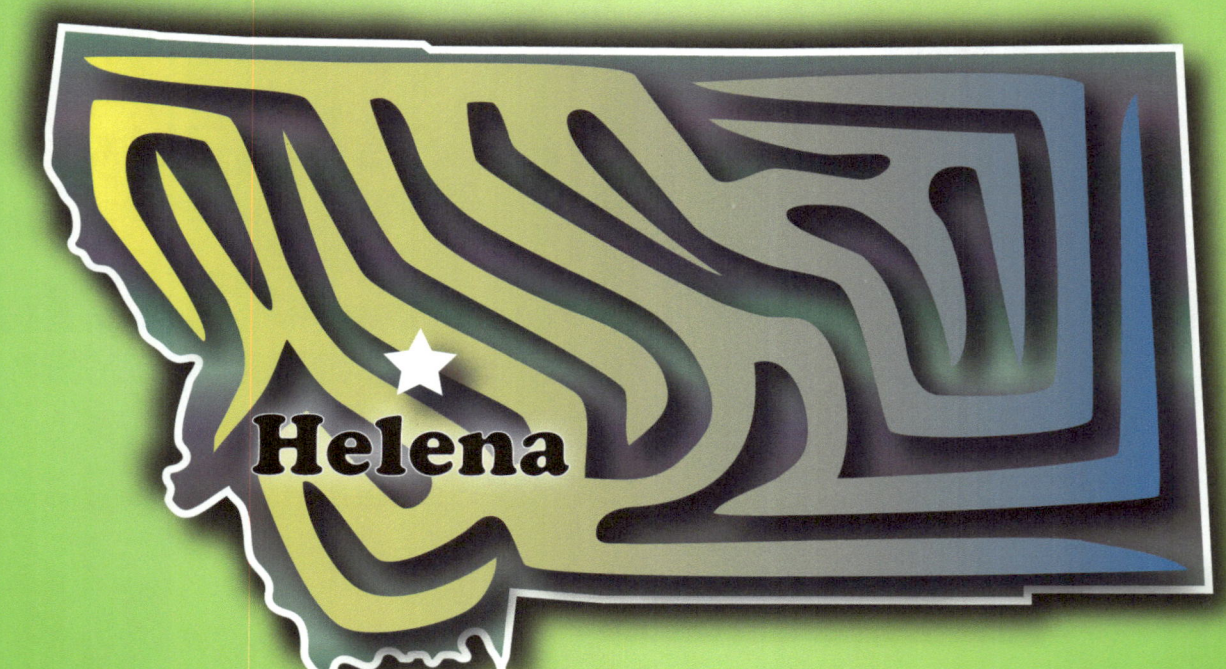

Helena

(MT)

MONTANA

26

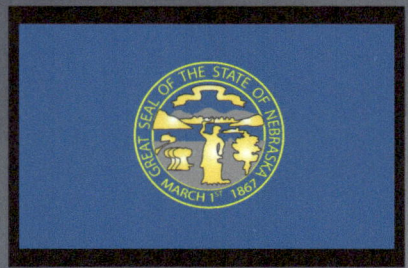

- Bellevue
- Columbus
- Fremont
- Grand Island
- Hastings
- Kearney

- La Vista
- Norfolk
- North Platte
- Omaha
- Papillion
- Scottsbluff

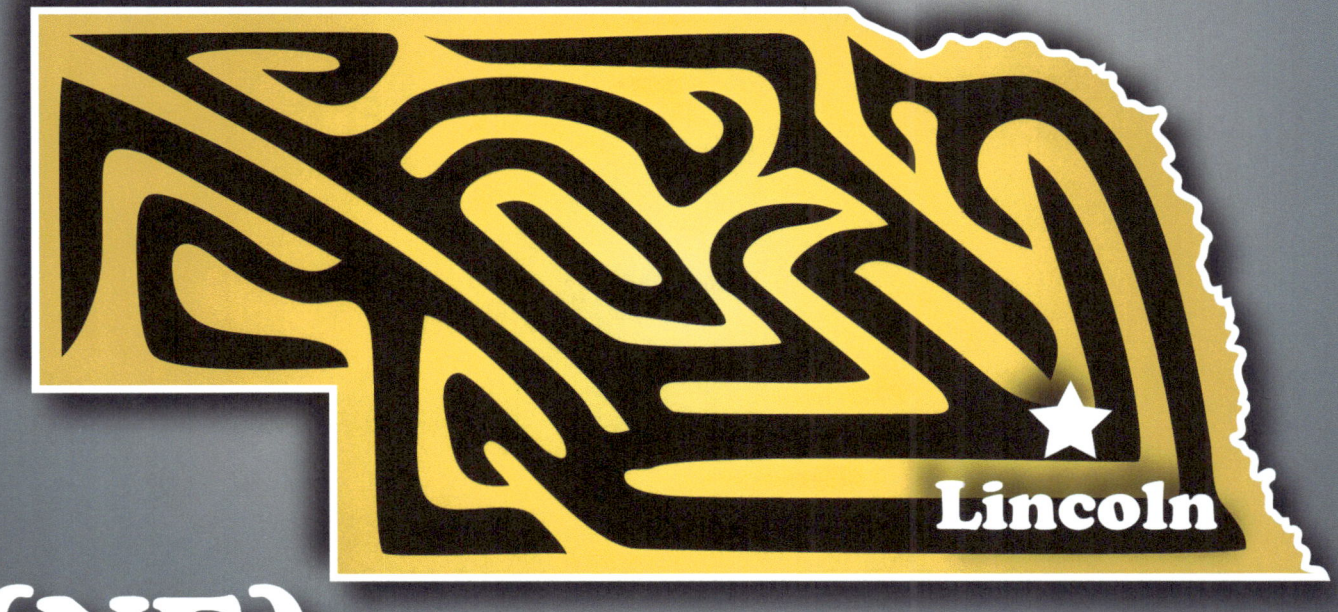

Lincoln

(NE)

NEBRASKA

27

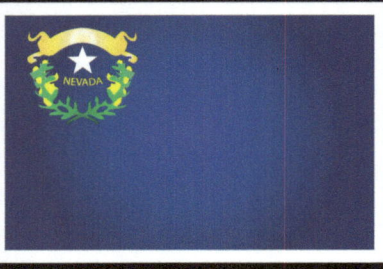

- Enterprise
- Henderson
- Las Vegas
- North Las Vegas
- Paradise
- Reno
- Sparks
- Spring Valley
- Sunrise Manor

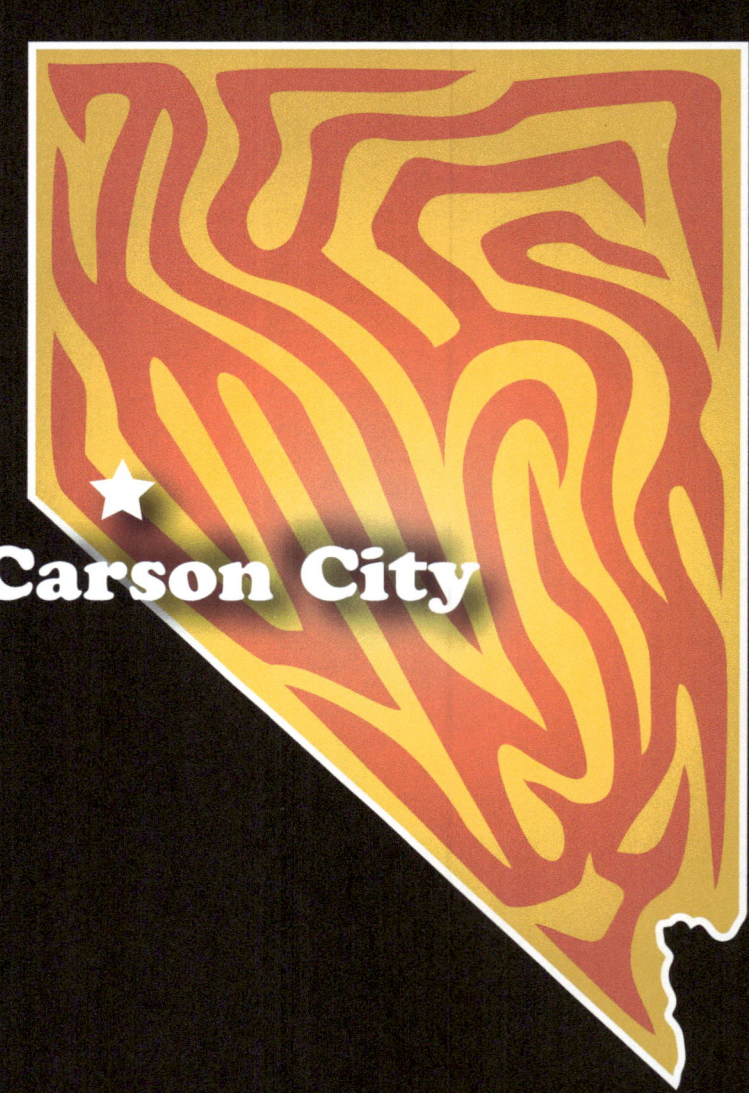

★ Carson City

(NV)

NEVADA

28

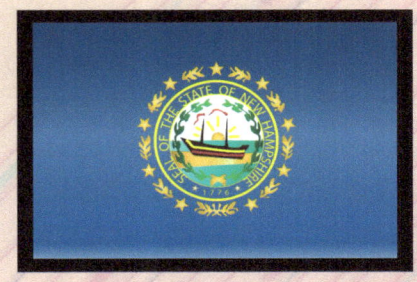

- Derry
- Dover
- Keene
- Laconia
- Manchester
- Nashua
- Portsmouth
- Rochester

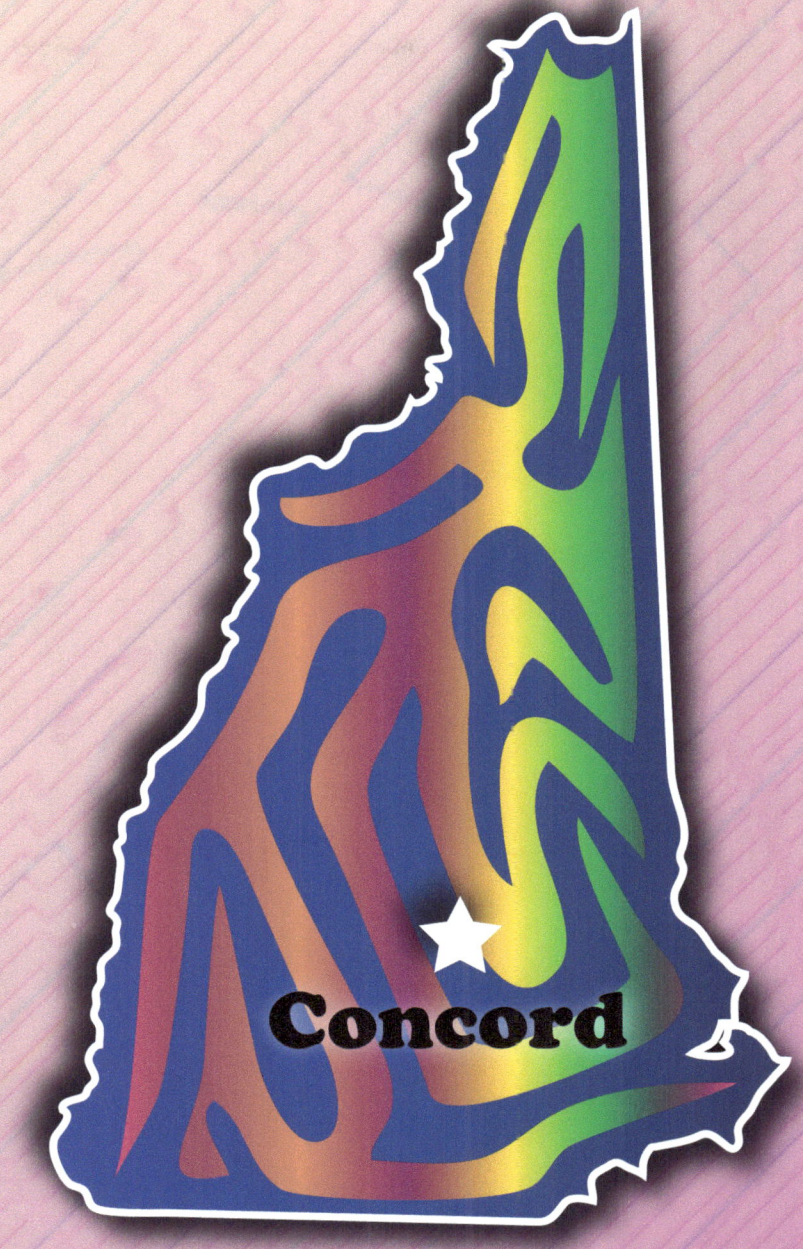

Concord

(NH)

NEW HAMPSHIRE

29

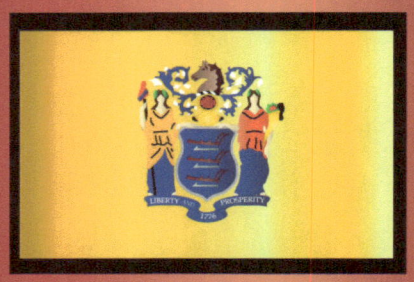

- **Brick Township**
- **Camden**
- **Clifton**
- **Edison**
- **Elizabeth**
- **Jersey City**
- **Newark**
- **Paterson**
- **Toms River**

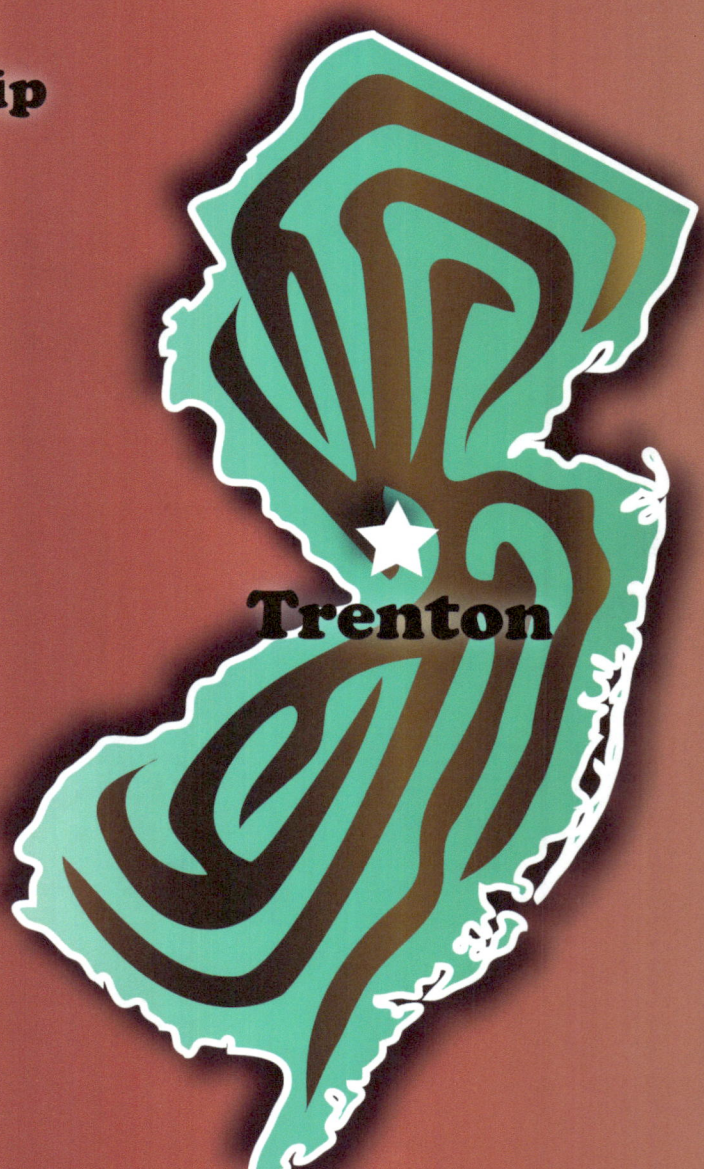

Trenton

(NJ)

30 NEW JERSEY

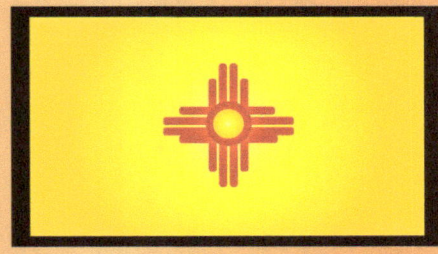

- Alamogordo
- Albuquerque
- Clovis
- Farmington
- Hobbs
- Las Cruces
- Rio Rancho
- Roswell
- South Valley

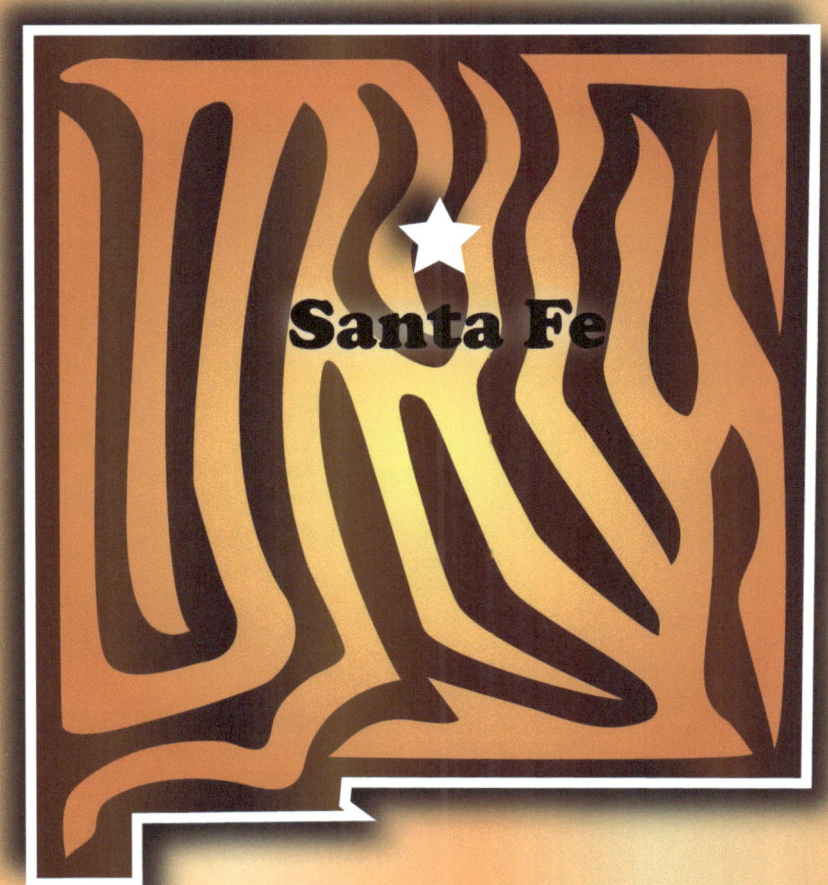

Santa Fe

(NM)

NEW MEXICO

31

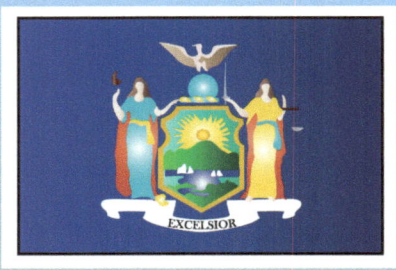

- **Buffalo**
- **Cheektowaga**
- **Mount Vernon**
- **New Rochelle**
- **New York**
- **Rochester**
- **Schenectady**
- **Syracuse**
- **Yonkers**

(NY)

32

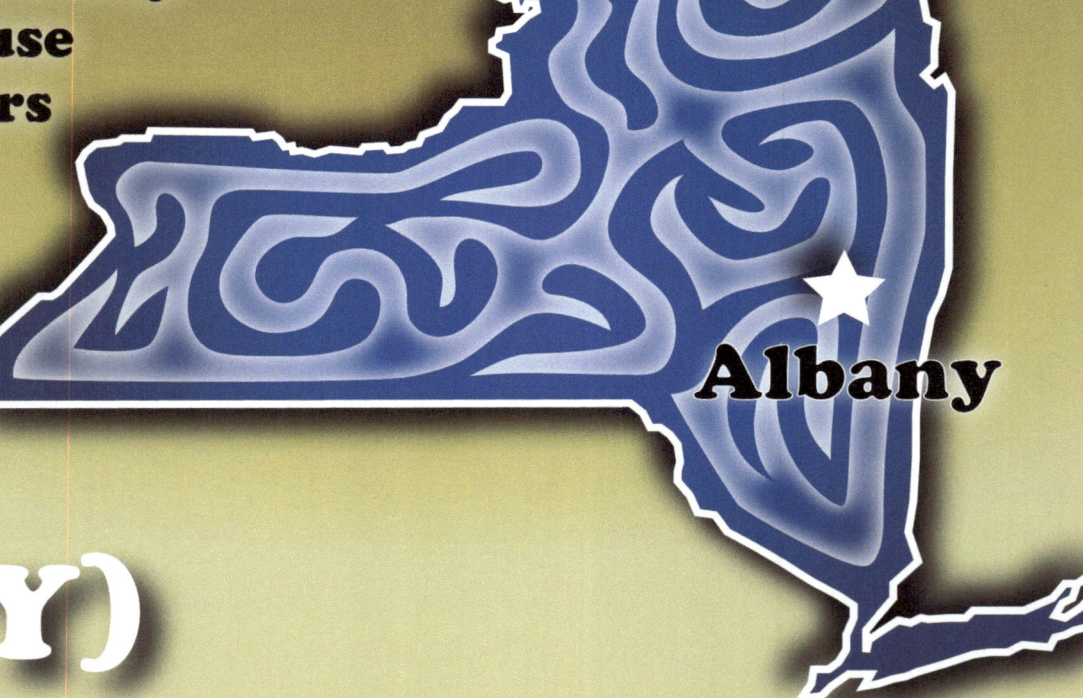

Albany

NEW YORK

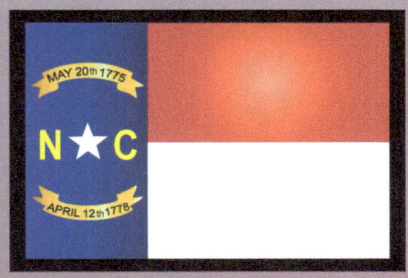

- Cary
- Charlotte
- Durham
- Fayetteville

- Greensboro
- High Point
- Wilmington
- Winston - Salem

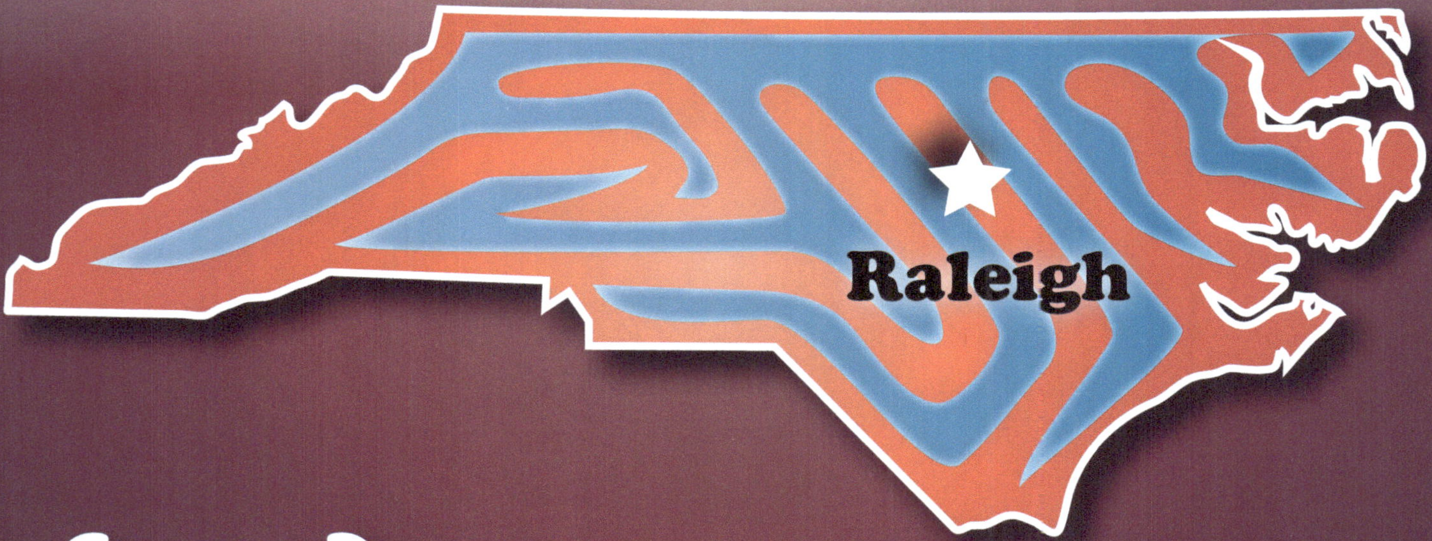

Raleigh

(NC)

NORTH CAROLINA

33

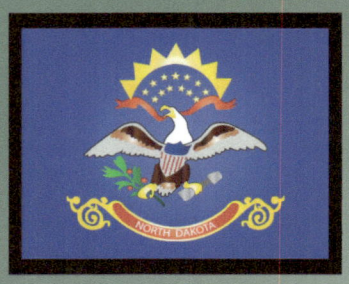

- Dickinson
- Fargo
- Grand Forks
- Jamestown
- Mandan
- Minot
- West Fargo
- Williston

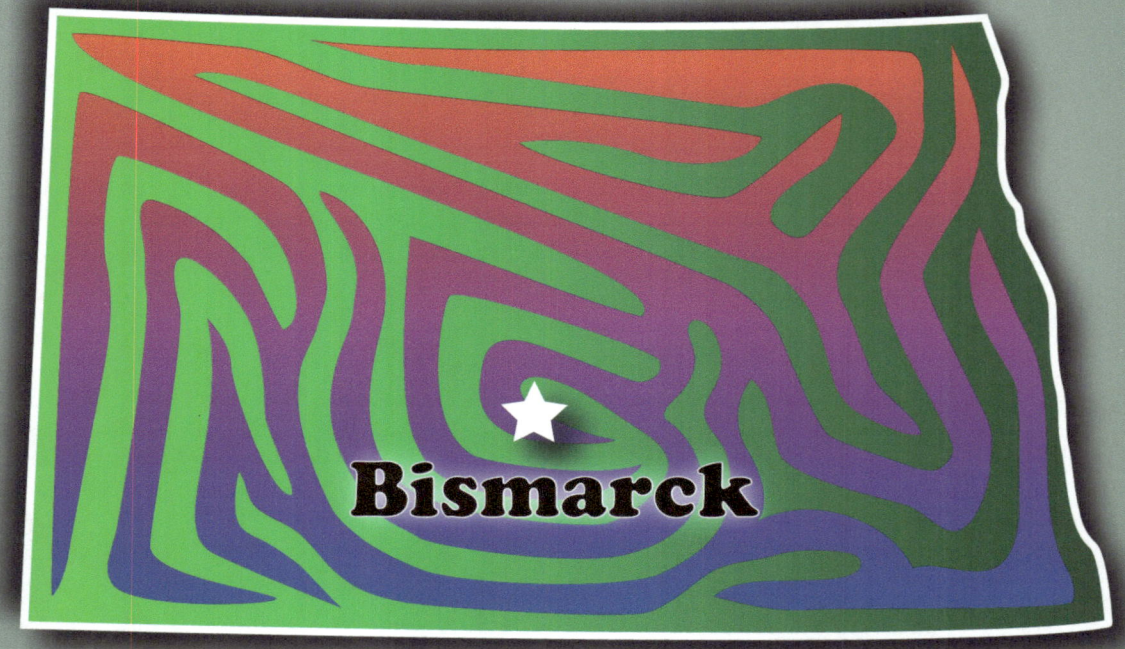

Bismarck

(ND)

NORTH DAKOTA

34

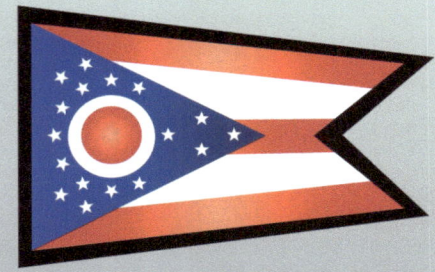

- Akron
- Canton
- Cleveland
- Cincinnati
- Dayton
- Lorian
- Parma
- Toledo
- Youngstown

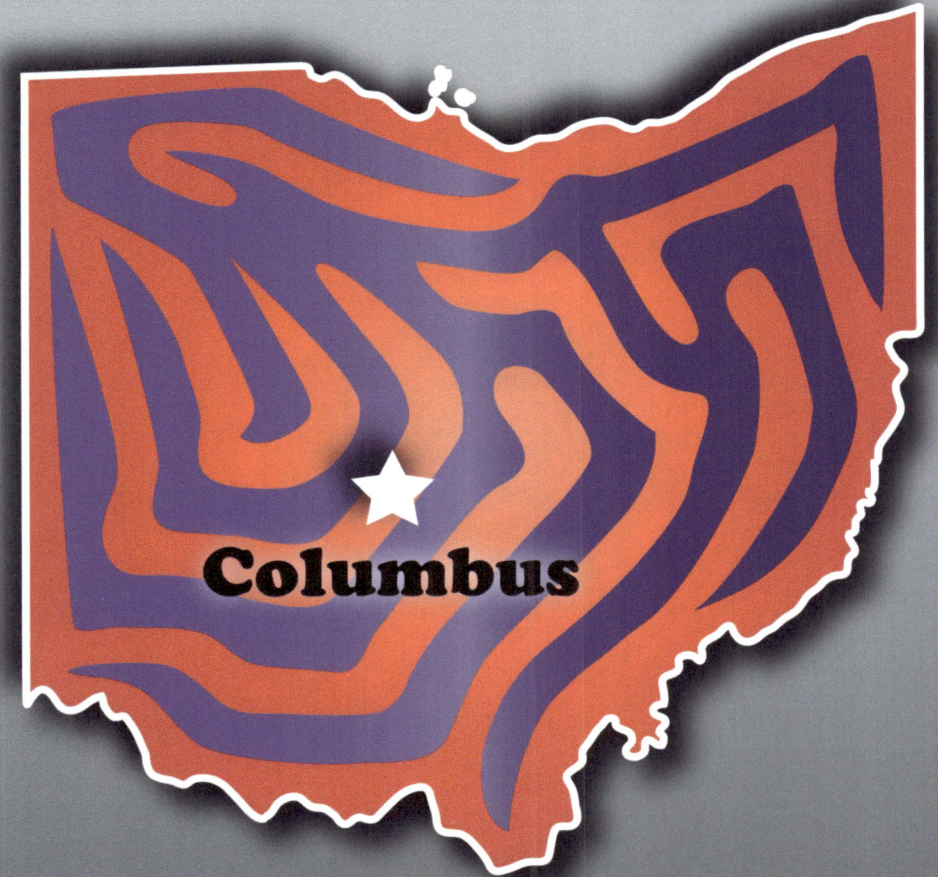

Columbus

(OH)

OHIO

35

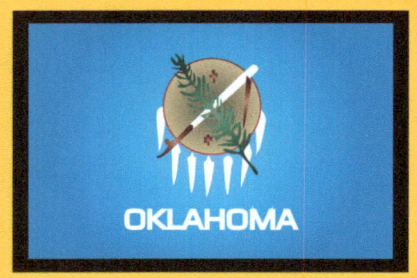

OKLAHOMA

- **Broken Arrow**
- **Edmond**
- **Enid**
- **Lawton**
- **Midwest City**
- **Moore**
- **Norman**
- **Stillwater**
- **Tulsa**

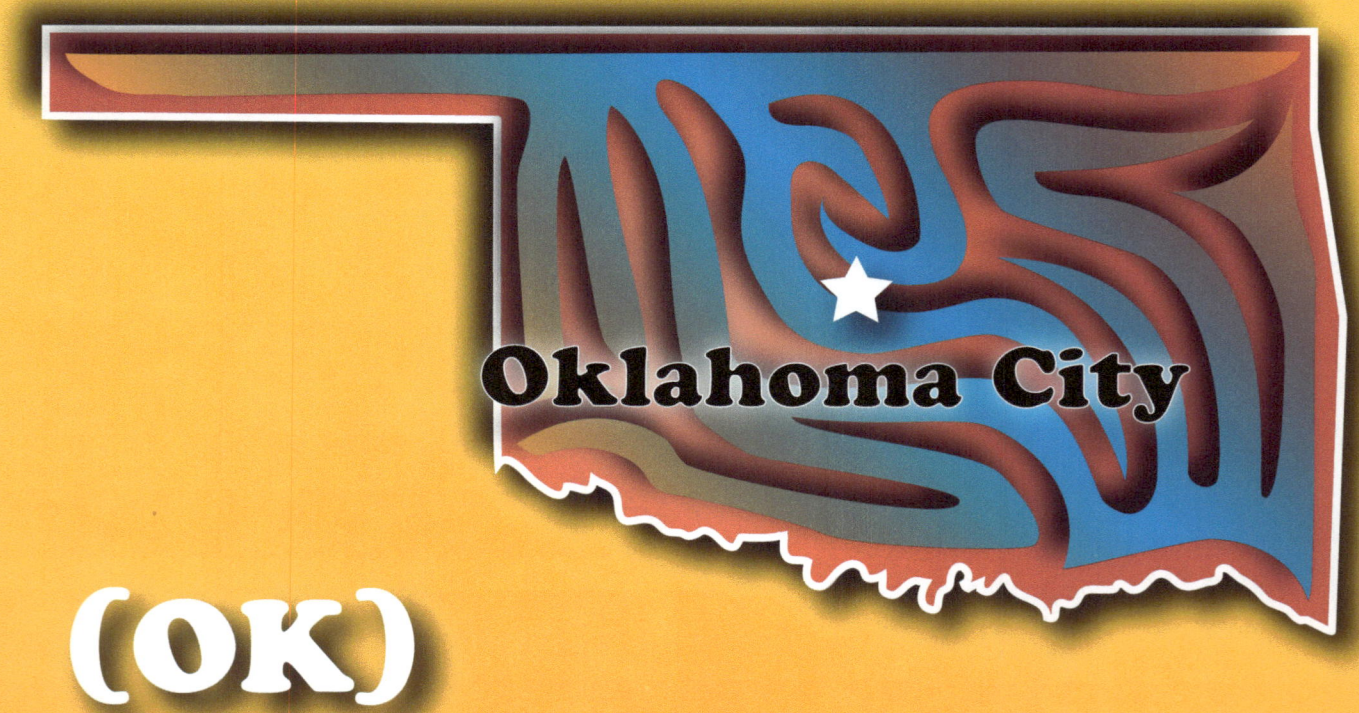

Oklahoma City

(OK)

OKLAHOMA

36

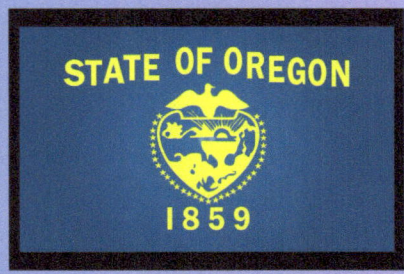

STATE OF OREGON

1859

- **Beaverton**
- **Bend**
- **Corvallis**
- **Eugene**
- **Gresham**

- **Hillsboro**
- **Medford**
- **Portland**
- **Springfield**

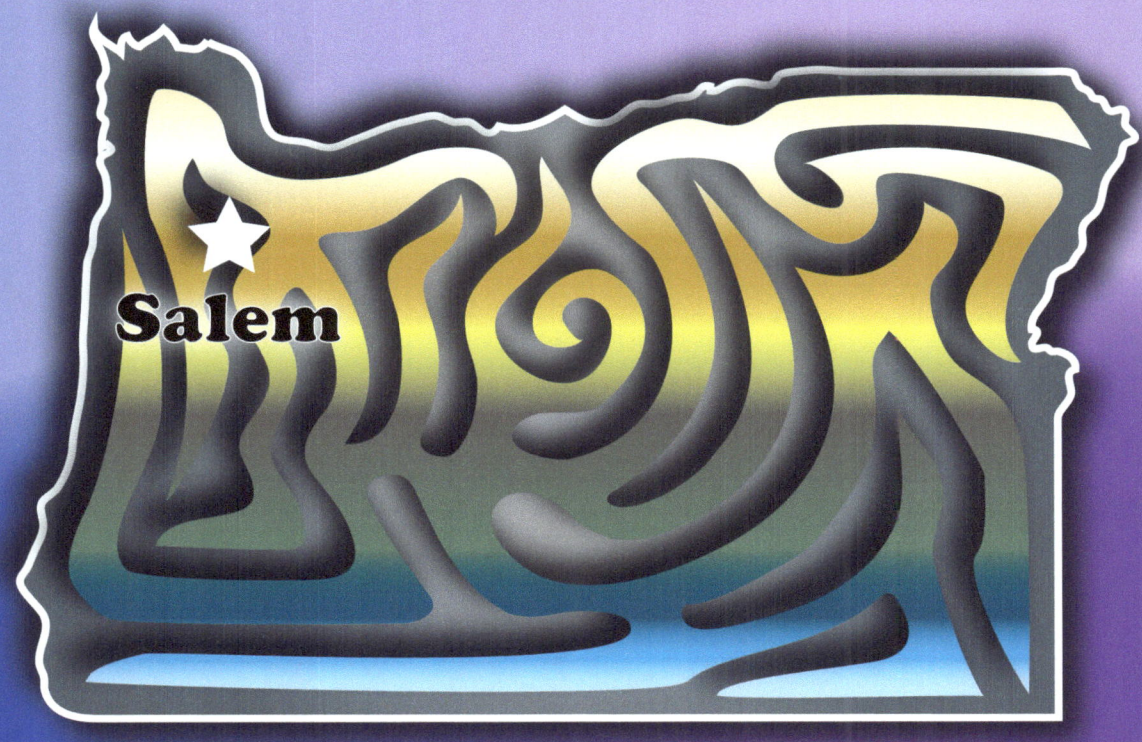

Salem

(OR)

OREGON

37

- Allentown
- Bethlehem
- Erie
- Lancaster
- Levittown

- Philadelphia
- Pittsburgh
- Reading
- Scranton

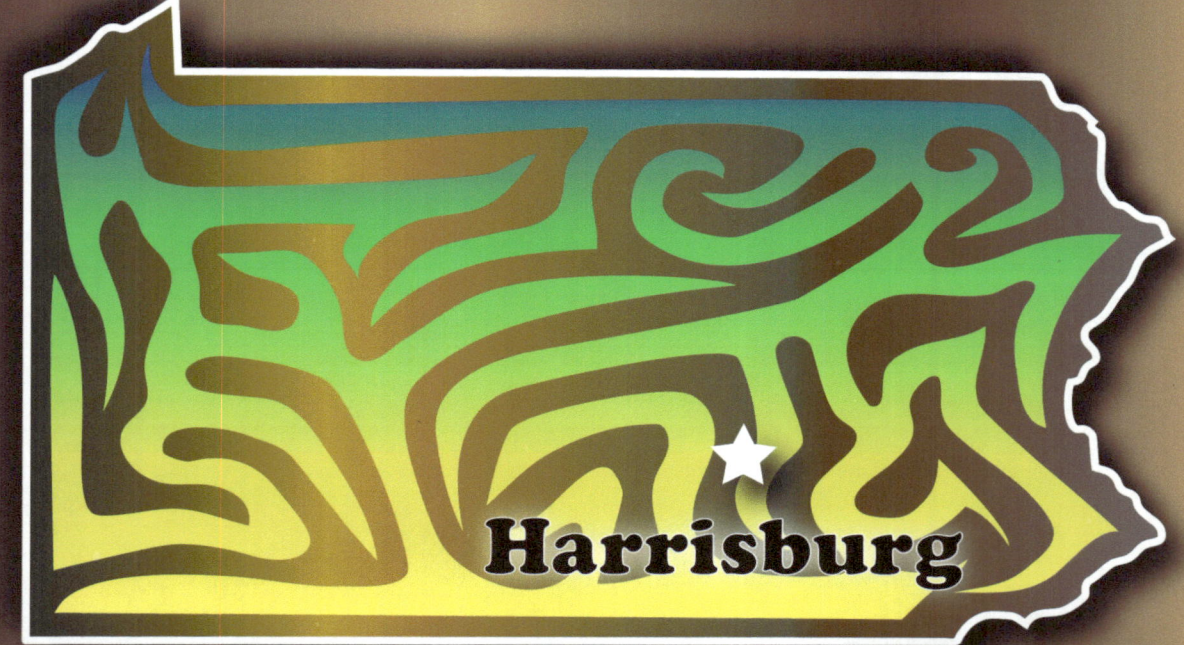

Harrisburg

(PA)
PENNSYLVANIA

38

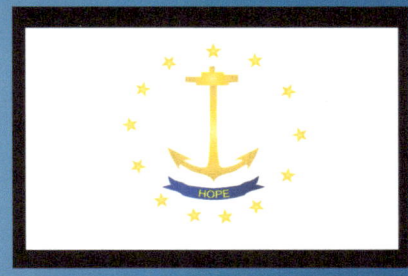

- Cranston
- Pawtucket
- Warwick

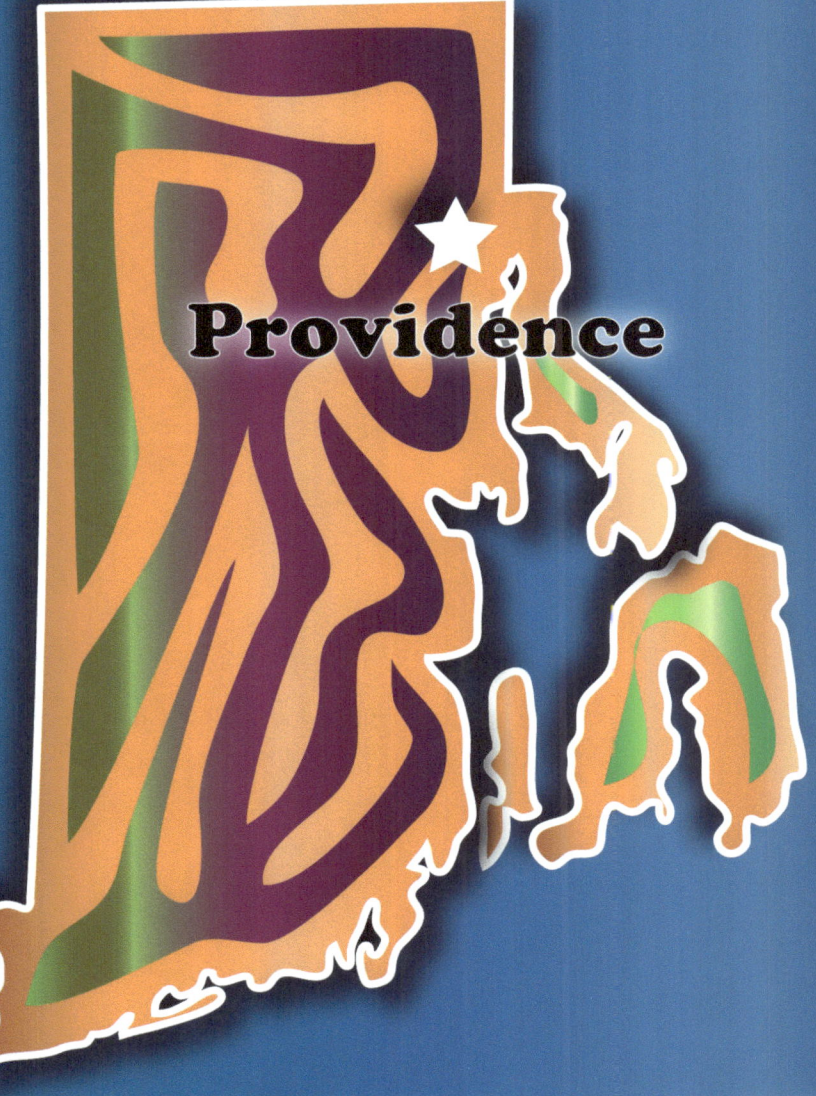

Providence

(RI)

RHODE ISLAND

39

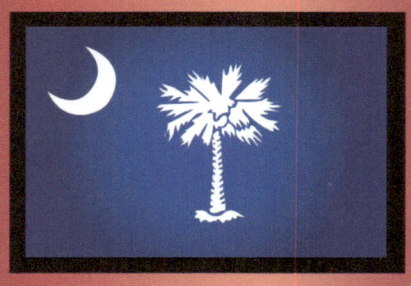

- Charleston
- Florence
- Greenville
- Goose Creek
- Hilton Head Island
- Mount Pleasant

- North Charleston
- Rock Hill
- Spartanburg
- Summerville
- Sumter

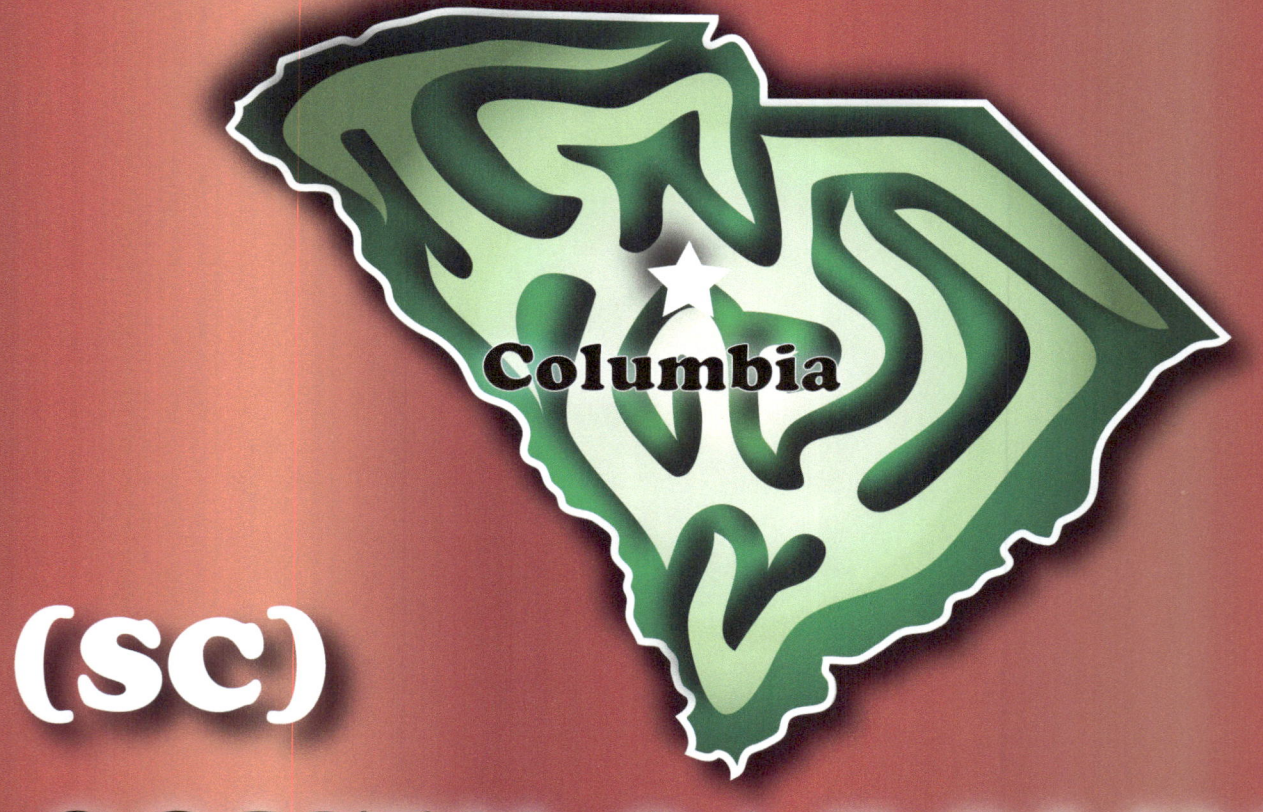

Columbia

(SC)

SOUTH CAROLINA
40

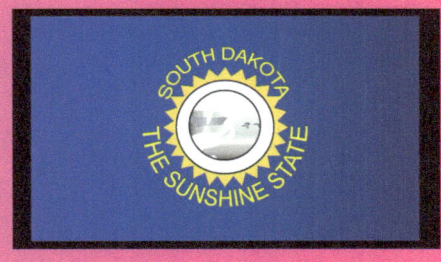

- Aberdeen
- Brookings
- Mitchell
- Rapid City
- Sioux Falls
- Watertown

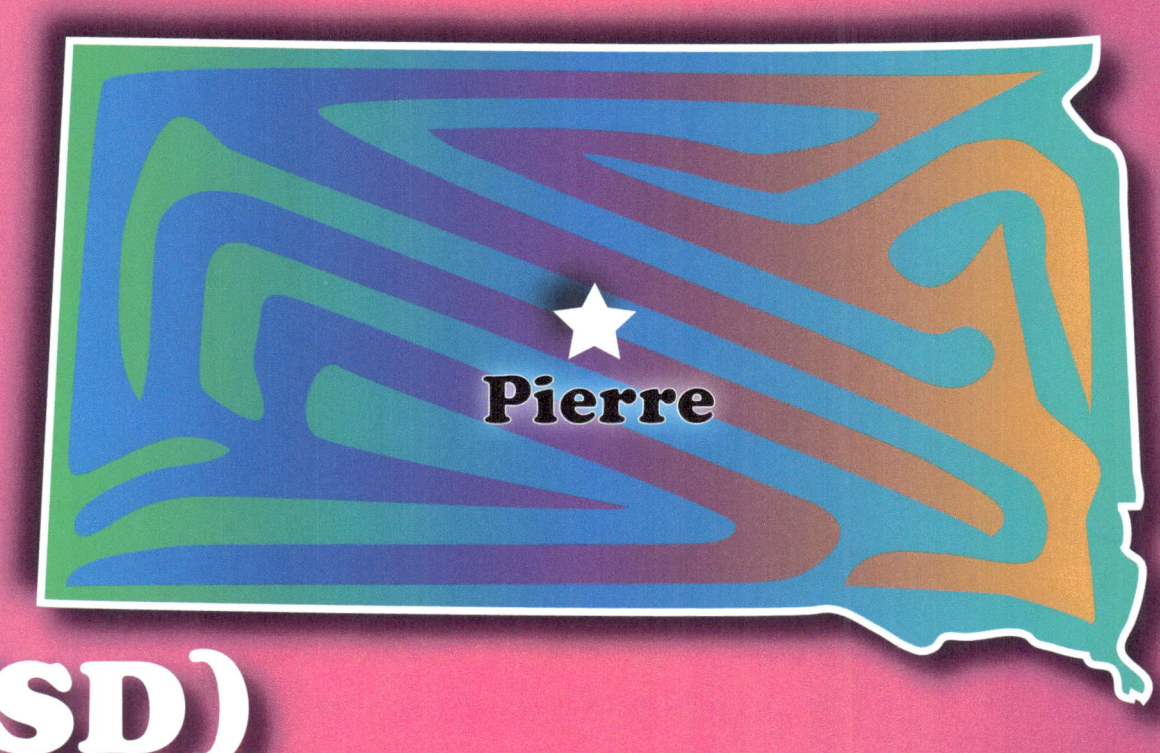

Pierre

(SD)
SOUTH DAKOTA
41

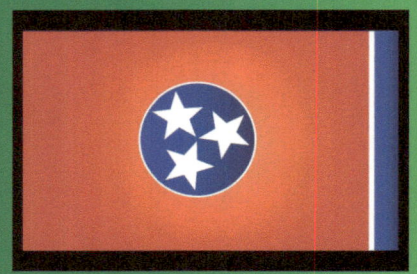

- Bartlett
- Chattanooga
- Clarksville
- Franklin
- Hendersonville
- Jackson

- Johnson City
- Kingsport
- Knoxville
- Memphis
- Murfreesboro

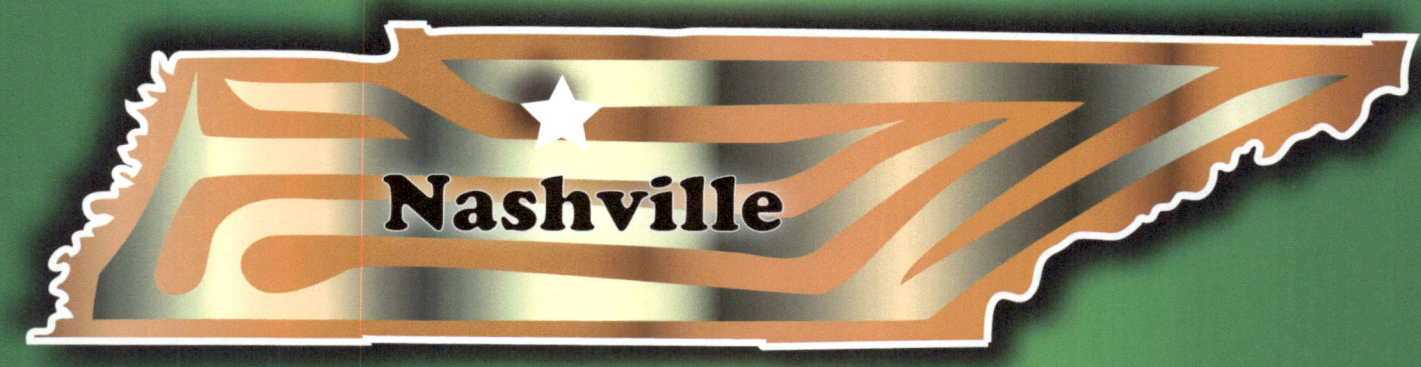

Nashville

(TN)

42

TENNESSE

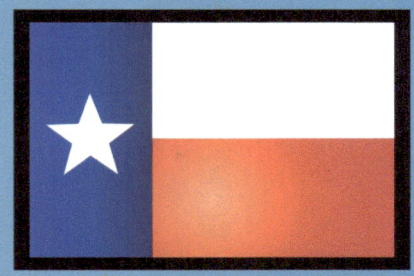

- **Arlington**
- **Corpus Christi**
- **Dallas**
- **El Paso**

- **Fort Worth**
- **Houston**
- **Plano**
- **San Antonio**

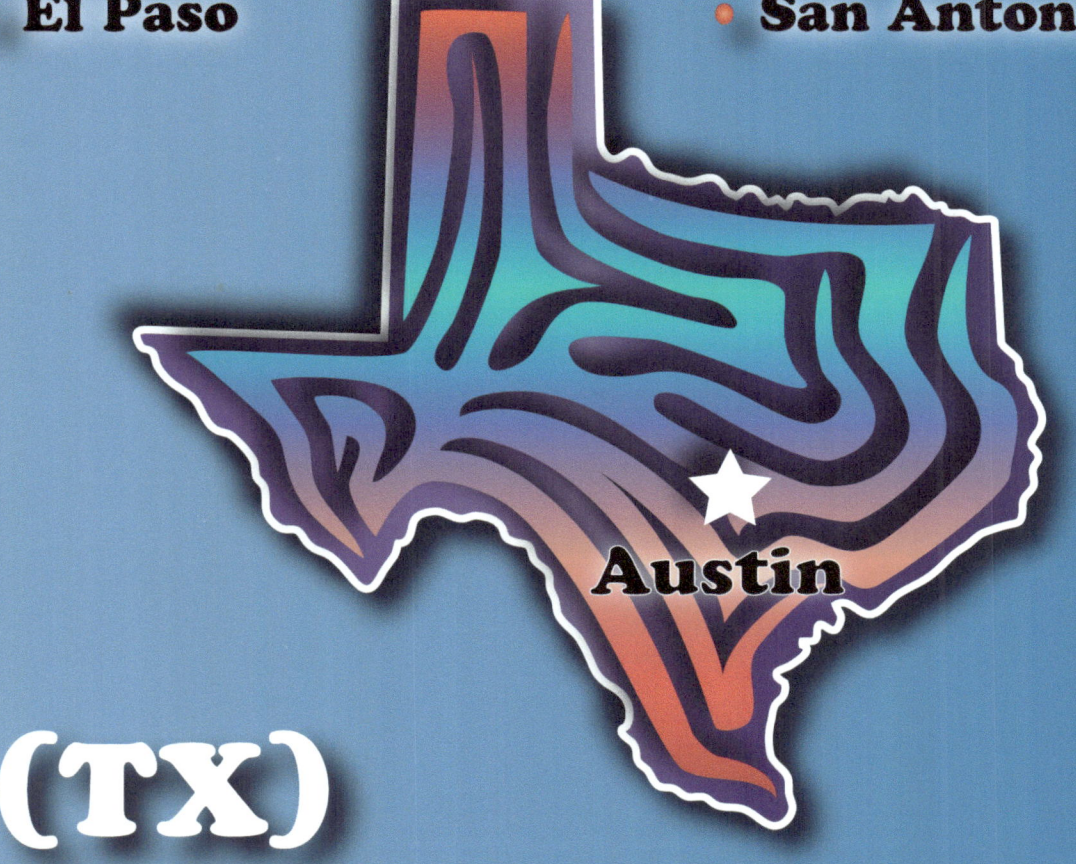

★ Austin

(TX)

TEXAS

43

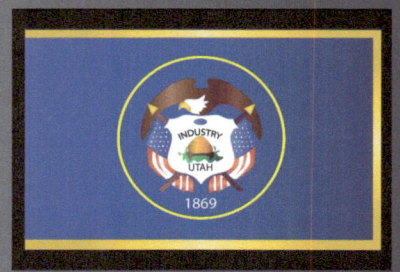

- Layton
- Ogden
- Orem
- Provo

- Sandy
- St. George
- West Jordan
- West Valley City

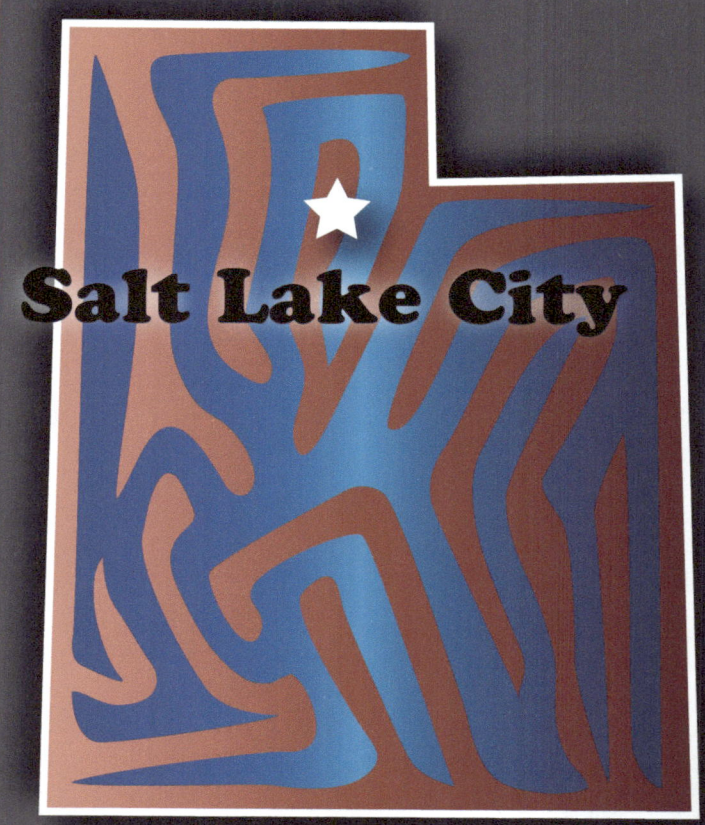

Salt Lake City

(UT)

UTAH

44

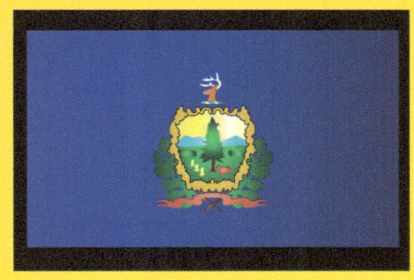

- **Burlington**
- **Rutland**
- **South Burlington**

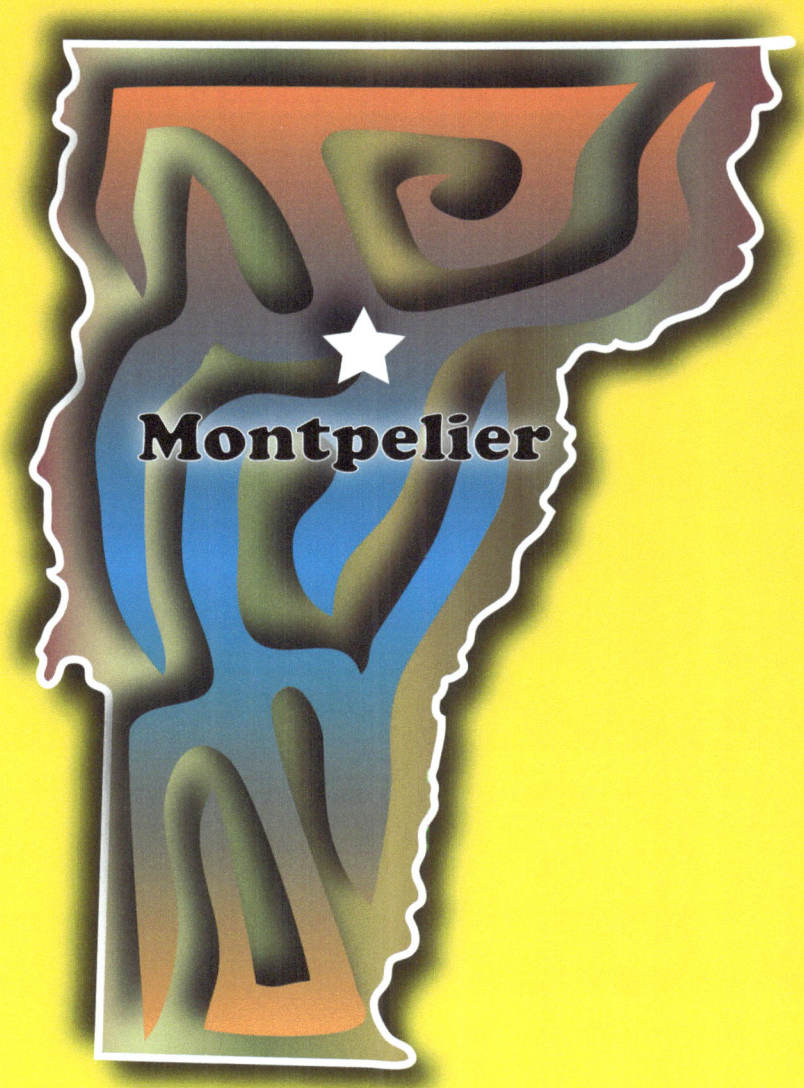

Montpelier

(VT)

VERMONT

45

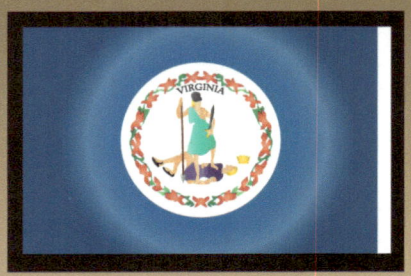

- Alexandria
- Arlington
- Chesapeake
- Hampton
- Newport News

- Norfolk
- Portsmouth
- Roanoke
- Virgina Beach

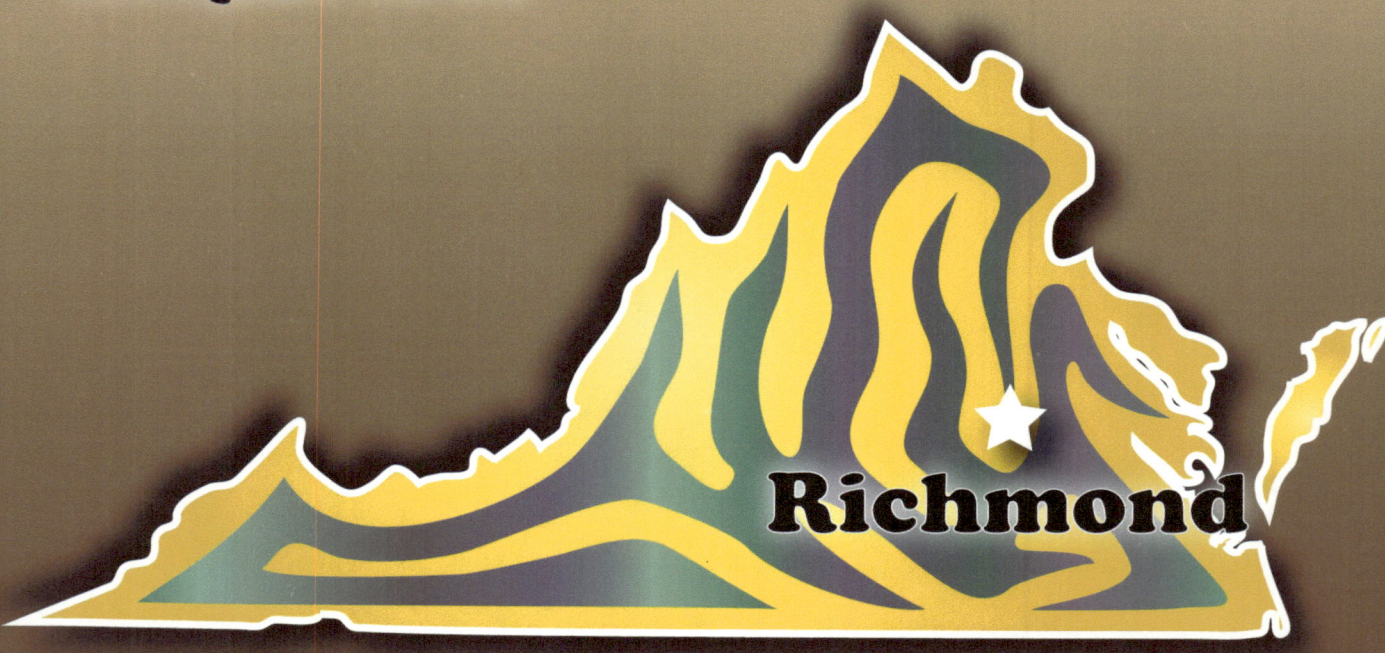

Richmond

(VA)

VIRGINIA

46

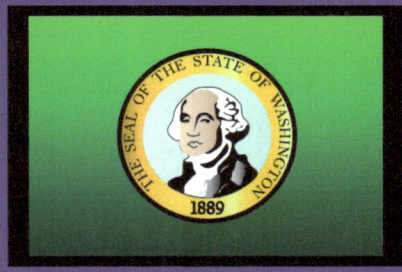

- Bellevue
- Everett
- Federal Way
- Kent
- Renton
- Seattle

- Spokane
- Spokane Valley
- Tacoma
- Vancouver
- Yakima

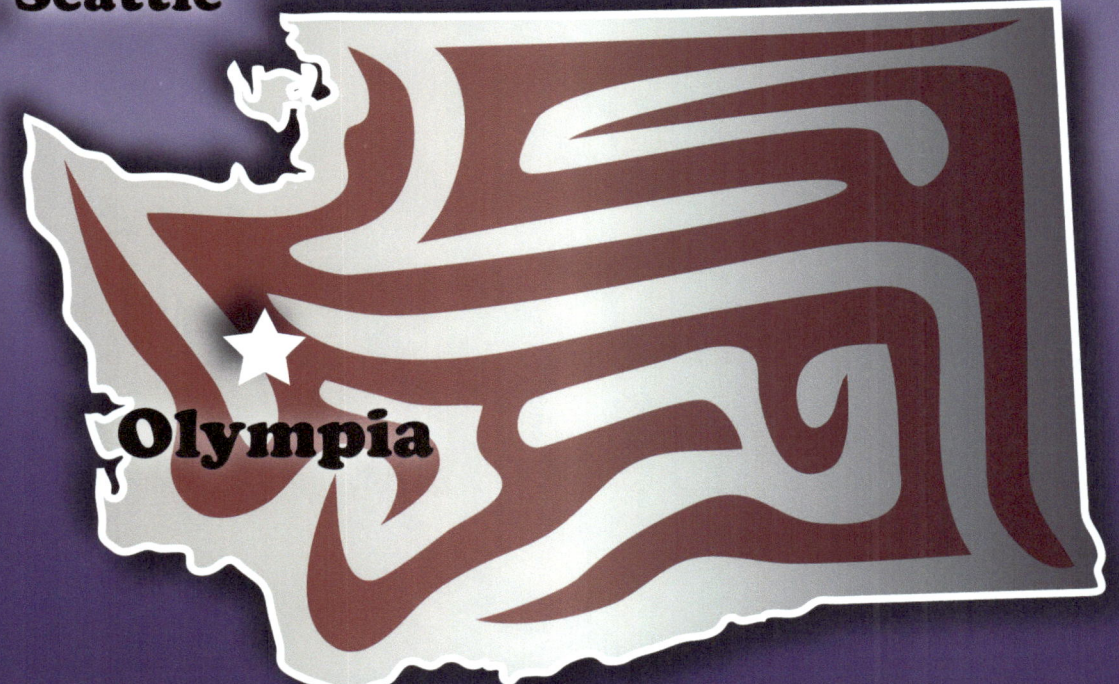

Olympia

(WA)
WASHINGTON

47

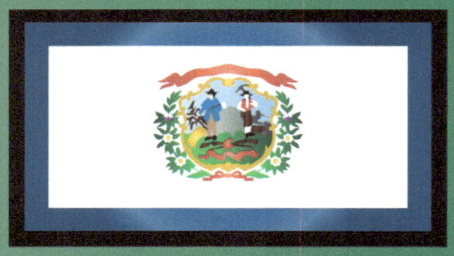

- Beckley
- Clarksburg
- Fairmont
- Huntington
- Martinsburg
- Morgantown
- Parkersburg
- Weirton
- Wheeling

Charleston

(WV)
WEST VIRGINIA
48

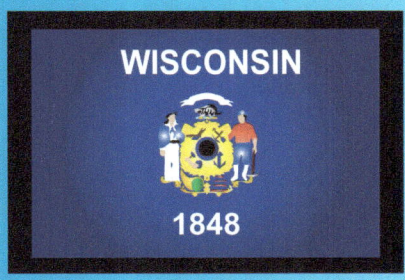

- **Appleton**
- **Eau Claire**
- **Green Bay**
- **Janesville**
- **Kenosha**
- **Milwaukee**
- **Oshkosh**
- **Racine**
- **Waukesha**
- **West Allis**

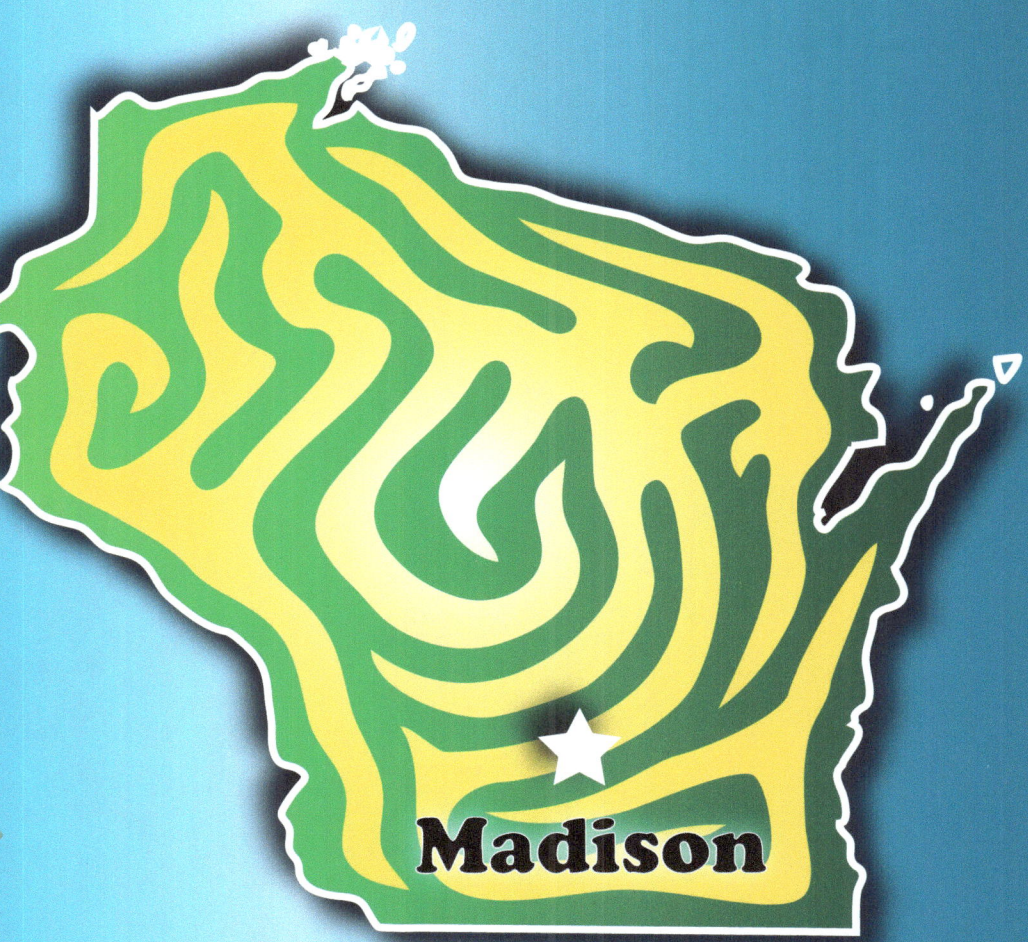

(WI)

WISCONSIN

49

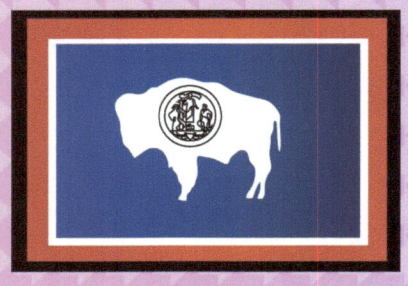

- Casper
- Gillette
- Laramie
- Rock Springs
- Sheridan

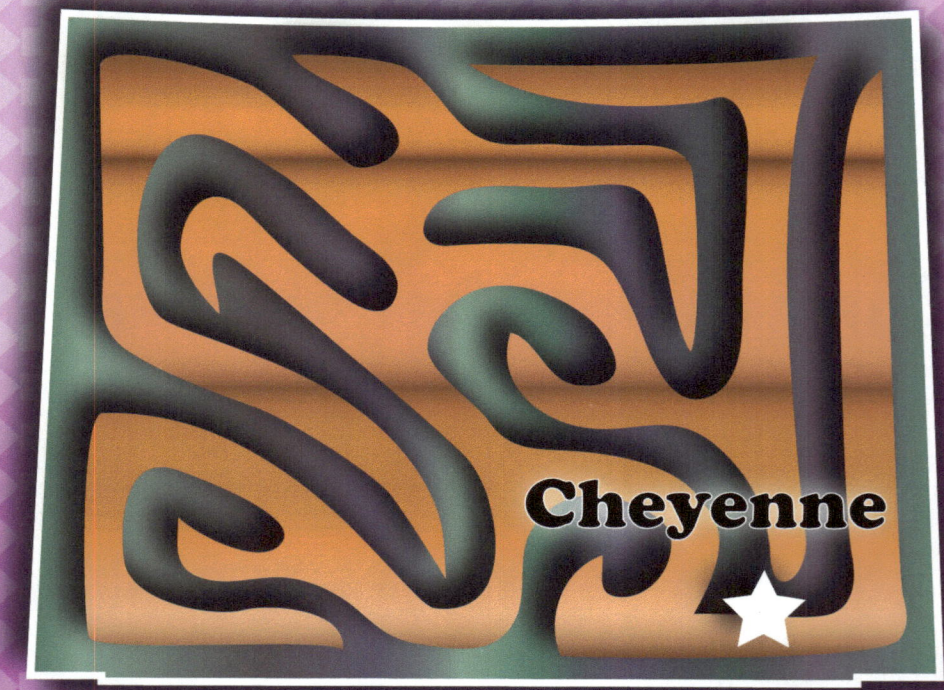

Cheyenne

(WY)

WYOMING

50